THE YEAR OF DREAMING DANGEROUSLY

THE YEAR OF DREAMING DANGEROUSLY

Slavoj Žižek

VERSO
London • New York

First published by Verso 2012
© Slavoj Žižek 2012

1 3 5 7 9 10 8 6 4 2

Verso
UK: 6 Meard Street, London W1F 0EG
US: 20 Jay Street, Suite 1010, Brooklyn, NY 11201

www.versobooks.com

Verso is the imprint of New Left Books

ISBN-13: 978-1-78168-042-1

British Library Cataloguing in Publication Data
A catalogue record for this book is available from the British Library

Library of Congress Cataloging-in-Publication Data
Žižek, Slavoj.
The year of dreaming dangerously / by Slavoj Žižek.
p. cm.
Includes bibliographical references.
ISBN 978-1-78168-042-1 (pbk. : alk. paper) —
ISBN 978-1-78168-043-8 (ebook)
1. Social history—21st century. 2. Social conflict—
History—21st century. 3. Social change—History—
21st century. 4. Political participation. I. Title.
HN18.3.Z54 2012
303.4—dc23
2012021758

Typeset in Minion Pro by MJ Gavan, Truro, Cornwall
Printed and bound in the US by Maple Vail

Contents

CHAPTER ONE

Introduction:
War Nam Nihadan

There is a wonderful expression in Persian, *war nam nihadan*, which means "to murder somebody, bury his body, then grow flowers over the body to conceal it."[1] In 2011, we witnessed (and participated in) a series of shattering events, from the Arab Spring to the Occupy Wall Street movement, from the UK riots to Breivik's ideological madness. It was the year of dreaming dangerously, in both directions: emancipatory dreams mobilizing protesters in New York, on Tahrir Square, in London and Athens; and obscure destructive dreams propelling Breivik and racist populists across Europe, from the Netherlands to Hungary. The primary task of the hegemonic ideology was to neutralize the true dimension of these events: was not the predominant reaction of the media precisely a *war nam nihadan*? The media killed the radical emancipatory potential of the events or obfuscated their threat to democracy, and then grew flowers over the buried corpse. This is why it is so important to set the record straight, to locate the events of 2011 in the totality of the global situation, to show how they relate to the central antagonism of contemporary capitalism.

Fredric Jameson argues that, in a determinate historical moment, the plurality of artistic styles or theoretical arguments can be sorted into tendencies that together form a system. To articulate such a system, Jameson as a rule relies on a Greimasian semiotic square, and for good reason: this square is not a purely formal structural matrix,

---

1   See Adam Jacot de Boinod, *The Meaning of Tingo*, London: Penguin Press 2005.

since it always starts with some basic opposition (antagonism or "contradiction"), and then looks for ways to displace and/or mediate the two opposed poles. The system of possible positions is thus a dynamic scheme of all possible answers or reactions to some basic structural deadlock or antagonism. This system does not simply limit the scope of the subject's freedom: it simultaneously opens up a space; in other words, it is "at one and the same time freedom and determination: it opens a set of creative possibilities (which are alone possible as responses to the situation it articulates) as well as tracing ultimate limits of praxis that are also the limits of thought and imaginative projection."[2] Jameson also raises the key epistemological question: such a system of all possible positions

> wants to be objective but can never be anything more than ideological: for [example in architecture] it becomes very difficult indeed to think how we might distinguish the real existence of the various kinds into which modern building falls from the patent invention of various systems of those kinds in our own heads. There is, in fact, something of a false problem here: the nagging worry, about whether we are in fact drawing our own eye, can be assuaged to a certain degree by the reminder that our eye is itself part of the very system of Being that is our object of speculation.[3]

Here, we are fully justified in following Hegel: if reality does not fit our concept, so much the worse for reality. Our scheme, if adequate, locates the formal matrix which is (imperfectly) followed by reality. As Marx already recognized, the "objective" determinations of social reality are at the same time "subjective" thought-determinations (of the subjects caught up in this reality), and, at this point of indistinction (at which the limits of our thought, its deadlocks and contradictions, are at the same time the antagonisms of objective social reality itself), "the diagnosis is also its own symptom."[4] Our diagnosis (our "objective" rendering of the system of all possible positions which determines the scope of our activity) is itself "subjective," it is a scheme of subjective reactions to a deadlock we confront in our practice and, in that sense,

---

2   Fredric Jameson, *Seeds of Time*, New York: Columbia University Press 1996, pp. 129–30.

3   Ibid., p. 130.

4   Ibid.

is symptomatic of this unresolved deadlock itself. Where we should nonetheless disagree with Jameson is in his designation of this indistinction of subjective and objective as "ideological": it is ideological only if we naively define "non-ideological" in terms of a purely "objective" description, a description free of all subjective involvement. But would it not be more appropriate to characterize as "ideological" any view that ignores not some "objective" reality undistorted by our subjective investment but *the very cause of this unavoidable distortion*, the real of that deadlock to which we react in our projects and engagements?

The present book endeavors to contribute to such a "cognitive mapping" (Jameson) of our constellation. After offering a brief description of the main features of today's capitalism, it goes on to outline the contours of its hegemonic ideology, focusing on the reactionary phenomena (populist revolts in particular) that arise in reaction to social antagonisms. The second half of the book deals with the two great emancipatory movements of 2011—the Arab Spring and Occupy Wall Street—before confronting, via a discussion of *The Wire*, the difficult question of how to fight the system without contributing to its enhanced functioning.

The instrument of such an account is what Immanuel Kant called the "public use of reason." Today, more than ever, one should bear in mind that Communism begins with the "public use of reason," with thinking, with the egalitarian universality of thought. For Kant, the public space of the "world-civil-society" designates the paradox of the universal singularity, of a singular subject who, in a kind of short-circuit, bypassing the mediation of the particular, directly participates in the Universal. This is what Kant, in the famous passage from his essay "What Is Enlightenment?", means by "public" as opposed to "private": the latter refers not to one's individual, as opposed to communal, ties, but to the very communal-institutional order of one's particular identification; while "public" designates the trans-national universality of the exercise of one's Reason.

However, does not this dualism of the public and private use of reason rely on what, in more contemporary terms, we could call the suspension of the symbolic efficacy (or performative power) of the public use of reason? Kant does not reject the standard formula of obedience—"Don't think, obey!"—in favor of its direct "revolutionary" opposite—"Don't obey [do what others tell you to do], think [with your own head]!". His formula is rather "Think and obey!"; that is, think publicly (with the free use of Reason) and obey privately (as part of the hierarchical machinery of power). In short, thinking freely does not authorize me to do just anything. The most I can do when my "public use of reason" leads me to see the weaknesses and injustices of the existing order is to make an appeal to the ruler for reforms. One can even go a step further here and claim, like Chesterton, that the abstract freedom to think (and doubt) actively prevents actual freedom:

> We may say broadly that free thought is the best of all the safeguards against freedom. Managed in a modern style the emancipation of the slave's mind is the best way of preventing the emancipation of the slave. Teach him to worry about whether he wants to be free, and he will not free himself.[5]

But is the subtraction of thinking from acting, the suspension of its efficiency, really as clear and unequivocal as that? Kant's secret strategy here (intentional or not) is like the well-known trick of the lawyer who makes a statement to the jury that he knows the judge will find inadmissible and order the jury to "ignore"—which is, of course, impossible, since the damage has already been done. Is not the withdrawal from efficacy in the public use of reason also a subtraction which opens up a space for some new social practice? It is all too easy to point out the obvious difference between the Kantian public use of reason and the Marxist notion of revolutionary class consciousness: the former is neutral and disengaged; the latter is "partial" and fully engaged. But the "proletarian position" can be defined precisely as that point at which the public use of reason becomes in itself practical and efficacious without regressing into the "privacy" of the private use of reason, since the position from which it is exercised is that of the "part of no-part" of the social body, its excess which stands directly for universality. By contrast, the Stalinist reduction of Marxist theory to the servant of the party-state is precisely a reduction of the public to the private use of reason.

Only such an approach which combines the universality of the

5   G.K. Chesterton, *Orthodoxy*, San Francisco: Ignatius Press 1995, p. 45.

"public use of reason" with an engaged subjective position can offer an adequate "cognitive mapping" of our situation. As Lenin put it: "We must *aussprechen was ist*, 'state the facts,' admit the truth that there is a tendency..." What tendency? Which facts are to be stated with regard to global capitalism today?

CHAPTER TWO

From Domination to Exploitation and Revolt

As Marxists, we share the premise that Marx's "critique of political economy" remains the starting point for understanding our socio-economic predicament. In order to grasp the specificity of that predicament, however, we must get rid of the last vestiges of Marx's evolutionary historicism—even if it appears to be the very foundation of Marxist orthodoxy. Here is Marx at his historicist worst:

> In the social production of their existence, men inevitably enter into definite relations, which are independent of their will, namely relations of production appropriate to a given stage in the development of their material forces of production ... At a certain stage of development, the material productive forces of society come into conflict with the existing relations of production or—this merely expresses the same thing in legal terms—with the property relations within the framework of which they have operated hitherto. From forms of development of the productive forces these relations turn into their fetters. Then begins an era of social revolution ... No social order is ever destroyed before all the productive forces for which it is sufficient have been developed, and new superior relations of production never replace older ones before the material conditions for their existence have matured within the framework of the old society. Mankind thus inevitably sets itself only such tasks as it is able to solve, since closer examination will always show that the problem itself arises only when the material conditions for its solution are already present or at least in the course of formation.[1]

---

1   Karl Marx, "Preface to A Contribution to the Critique of Political

This schema is doubly wrong. First, capitalism as a social formation is characterized by a structural imbalance: the antagonism between forces and relations is present from the very beginning, and it is this very antagonism which pushes capitalism towards permanent self-revolutionizing and self-expansion—capitalism thrives because it avoids its fetters by escaping into the future. This is also why one has to drop the "wisely" optimistic notion that mankind "inevitably sets itself only such tasks as it is able to solve": today we face problems for which no clear solutions are guaranteed by the logic of evolution.

In order to move beyond this frame, we should focus on the three features that characterize contemporary capitalism: the long-term trend of shifting from profit to rent (in its two main forms: rent based on privatized "common knowledge," and rent based on natural resources); the much stronger structural role of unemployment (the opportunity to be "exploited" in a long-term job is experienced as a privilege); and finally the rise of a new class that Jean-Claude Milner calls the "salaried bourgeoisie."[2]

The consequence of the rise in productivity brought about by an exponential growth in collective knowledge is the changing role of unemployment. But does this new form of capitalism not also offer a new prospect of emancipation? Therein lies the thesis of Hardt and Negri's *Multitude*, in which they endeavor to radicalize a Marx for whom highly organized corporate capitalism already was "socialism within capitalism" (a kind of socialization of capitalism, with the absent owners becoming more and more superfluous), so that one only need cut off the nominal head to reach socialism proper.[3] For Hardt and Negri, however, Marx's limitation was that he was historically constrained by the centralized and hierarchically organized form of industrial labor, which is why his vision of the "general intellect" was that of a central planning agency. It is only today, with the rise of "immaterial labor" to a hegemonic position, that the revolutionary reversal becomes "objectively possible." This immaterial labor extends between the two poles of intellectual (symbolic) labor (the production of ideas, codes, texts, programs, figures...) and affective labor

---

Economy" (1859), *Selected Writings*, ed. Lawrence H. Simon, Indianapolis: Hackett 1994, p. 211.

2 See Jean-Claude Milner, *Clartés de tout*, Paris: Verdier 2011.

3 Michael Hardt and Antonio Negri, *Multitude*, New York: Penguin 2004.

(those who deal with our bodily affects: from doctors to baby-sitters and flight attendants). Today, immaterial labor is "hegemonic" in the precise sense in which Marx proclaimed that, in nineteenth-century capitalism, large industrial production was hegemonic as the specific color lending its tone to the totality—not in quantitative terms, but playing the key, emblematic and structural role. What thereby emerges is a vast new domain of the "common": shared knowledge, forms of cooperation and communication, etc., which can no longer be contained by the form of private property. For, in immaterial production, the products are no longer material objects, but new social (interpersonal) relations themselves—in short, immaterial production is directly biopolitical, it is the production of social life.

The irony here is that Hardt and Negri are referring to the very process that the ideologists of today's "postmodern" capitalism celebrate as the passage from material to symbolic production, from a centralist-hierarchical logic to the logic of autopoietic self-organization, multi-centered cooperation, and so on. Negri is indeed faithful to Marx here: what he tries to prove is that Marx was right, that the rise of the "general intellect" is in the long term incompatible with capitalism. The ideologists of postmodern capitalism make exactly the opposite claim: it is Marxist theory (and practice) itself which remains within the constraints of the hierarchical and centralized logic of state control and thus cannot cope with the social effects of the new information revolution. There are good empirical reasons for this claim: again, the supreme irony of history is that the disintegration of Communism is the most convincing example of the validity of the traditional Marxist dialectic of forces and relations of production, on which Marxism counted in its attempt to overcome capitalism. What indeed ruined the Communist regimes was their inability to accommodate the new social logic sustained by the "information revolution": they tried to steer it into yet another large-scale centralized state-planning project. The paradox is thus that what Negri celebrates as a unique opportunity for overcoming capitalism, the ideologists of the "information revolution" celebrate as the rise of a new "frictionless" capitalism.

Hardt and Negri's analysis has three weak points that, taken together, explain how capitalism can survive what should be (in classical Marxist terms) a new organization of production that renders it obsolete. They underestimate the extent to which contemporary capitalism successfully (in the short term at least) privatized "common knowledge" itself, as well as the extent to which, more so than the bourgeoisie, workers themselves are becoming "superfluous" (increasing numbers of them becoming not just temporarily unemployed, but structurally unemployable). Furthermore, even if it is in principle true that the bourgeoisie is becoming progressively non-functional, we should qualify this statement with the question non-functional *for whom? For capitalism itself.* That is to say, if the old capitalism ideally involved an entrepreneur investing (her own or borrowed) money into a venture organized and run by herself, thereby reaping the profit, a new ideal type is emerging today: no longer the entrepreneur who owns her own company, but the expert manager (or a managerial board presided over by a CEO) who runs a company owned by banks (also run by managers who do not own the bank itself) or dispersed investors. In this new ideal type of capitalism without the bourgeoisie, the old bourgeoisie, rendered non-functional, becomes re-functionalized as a class of salaried managers—the new bourgeoisie itself receives a salary, and even if its members own part of their company, they earn their stock as part of the remuneration for their work ("bonuses" for their "successful" management).

This new bourgeoisie still appropriates surplus-value, but in the (mystified) form of what Milner calls the "surplus-wage": in general, its members are paid more than the proletarian "minimum wage" (this imaginary—often mythical—point of reference whose only real example in today's global economy is the salary of a worker in a sweatshop in China or Indonesia), and it is this difference from common proletarians, this distinction, which determines their status. The bourgeoisie in the classic sense thus tend to disappear: capitalists reappear as a subset of salaried workers—managers who are qualified to earn more by their competence (which is why the pseudo-scientific "evaluation" which legitimizes their higher earnings is so crucial today). The category of workers earning a surplus-wage is, of course, not limited to managers: it is extended to all sorts of experts, administrators, public servants, doctors, lawyers, journalists, intellectuals, and artists. The surplus they receive has two forms: more money (for managers, and so on), but also less work, that is, more free time (for some intellectuals, but also for some members of the state administration, etcetera).

The evaluative procedure that qualifies some workers to receive a surplus-wage is, of course, an arbitrary mechanism of power and ideology, with no serious link to actual competence—or, as Milner puts it, the necessity of the surplus-wage is not economic, but political: to maintain a "middle class" for the purpose of social stability. The arbitrariness of the social hierarchy is not a mistake, but its whole point, for the arbitrariness of evaluation plays a role homologous to the arbitrariness of market success. In other words, violence threatens to explode not when there is too much contingency in the social sphere, but when one tries to eliminate this contingency.

Therein lies one of the impasses faced by China today: the goal of Deng's reforms was to introduce capitalism without a bourgeoisie (as the new ruling class); now, however, Chinese leaders are becoming painfully aware that capitalism without a stable hierarchy (brought by the bourgeoisie as a new class) generates permanent instability. So what path will China take? More generally, this is also arguably the reason why (ex-)Communists are re-emerging as the most efficient managers of capitalism: their historical enmity towards the bourgeoisie as a class fits perfectly with the progress of contemporary capitalism towards a managerial system without the bourgeoisie—in both cases, as Stalin put it long ago, "cadres decide everything."[4]

This notion of the surplus-wage also allows us to throw new light on the ongoing "anti-capitalist" protests. In times of crisis, the obvious candidates for a "tightening of belts" are the lower levels of the salaried bourgeoisie: since their surplus-wages play no immanent economic role, the only thing that stands in the way of their joining the proletarians is their power of political protest. Although these protests are nominally directed at the brutal logic of the market, they are in reality protesting the gradual erosion of their (politically) privileged economic position. Recall Ayn Rand's favorite ideological fantasy (from *Atlas Shrugged*), that of ("creative") capitalists going on strike—does this fantasy not find a perverted realization in many strikes today, which are often strikes of the privileged "salaried bourgeoisie" driven by the fear of losing their privileges (the surplus over the minimal

---

4   There is also an interesting difference emerging between today's China and Russia: in Russia, university cadres are ridiculously underpaid; they have de facto already joined the proletariat, while in China, they are well provided with a "surplus-wage" as a means to guarantee their docility.

wage)? They are not proletarian protests, but protests against the threat of being reduced to a proletarian status. In other words, who dares to strike today, when having the security of a permanent job is itself becoming a privilege? These are not the low-paid workers in (what remains of) the textile industry and so on, but that strata of privileged workers with guaranteed jobs (mostly in the civil service: police and other law enforcers, teachers, public transport workers, etcetera). This also accounts for the new wave of student protests: their main motivation is arguably the fear that higher education will no longer guarantee them a surplus-wage in later life.

Of course, the great revival of protest—from the Arab Spring to Western Europe, from Occupy Wall Street to China, from Spain to Greece—should not be dismissed as merely a revolt of the salaried bourgeoisie. It harbors a much more radical potential, one that requires a concrete, case-by-case analysis. The student protests against university reforms in the UK, for example, were clearly different from the UK riots of August 2011—that consumerist carnival of destruction, a genuine outburst from those excluded from the system. As to the uprising in Egypt, one could argue that it did begin as a revolt of the salaried bourgeoisie (the young and educated protesting at the lack of prospects), but quickly became part of a larger protest against an oppressive regime. But to what extent did the protest mobilize poor workers and peasants? Does not the electoral victory of the Islamists indicate the narrow social base of the original secular protest? Greece is a special case here: over the last few decades, a new salaried bourgeoisie (especially in the over-extended state administration) has been created, with EU financial help, and much of the ongoing protest is a response to the threat of losing these privileges.

This proletarianization of the lower salaried bourgeoisie is accompanied by an excess in the opposite direction: the irrationally high pay of top managers and bankers, a level of remuneration that is economically irrational since, as investigations in the US have demonstrated, it tends to be inversely proportional to the company's success.[5] Instead of submitting these trends to moralizing criticism, we should rather read them as indications of how the capitalist system

---

5   True, part of the price paid for this hyper-remuneration is that managers have to be available twenty-four hours a day, thus living in a permanent emergency state.

itself is no longer able to find an immanent level of self-regulated stability; that is, of how its circuit threatens to run out of control.

The good old Marxist-Hegelian notion of totality comes into its own here: it is crucial to grasp the ongoing economic crisis in its totality and not be blinded by its partial aspects. The first step towards grasping this totality is to focus on those singular moments that stick out as symptoms of the present economic predicament. For example, everyone knows that the "rescue package" for Greece will not work, but nonetheless new rescue packages are imposed on Greece over and over again in a weird example of the logic of "I know very well, but..." Two dominant stories about the Greek crisis circulate in the mass media: the German-European one (the irresponsible, lazy, free-spending, tax-dodging Greeks must be brought under control and taught financial discipline), and the Greek one (their national sovereignty is threatened by the neoliberal technocracy in Brussels).[6] When it became impossible to ignore the plight of ordinary Greeks, a third story emerged: they are increasingly presented as humanitarian victims in need of help, as if some natural catastrophe or war had hit the country. While all three stories are false, the third is arguably the most disgusting: it conceals the fact that the Greeks are not passive victims; they are fighting back, they are at war with the European economic establishment and what they need is solidarity in their struggle, because this is our fight as well. Greece is not an exception; it is a testing ground for the imposition of a new socio-economic model with a universal claim: the depoliticized technocratic model wherein bankers and other experts are allowed to squash democracy.

Imagine a scene from a dystopian movie depicting our society in the near future: ordinary people walking the streets carry a special whistle; whenever they see something suspicious—an immigrant,

---

6   One of Jacques Lacan's more outrageous statements is that even if a jealous husband's claim that his wife sleeps around turns out to be true, his jealousy is still pathological. Along the same lines, we could say that even if most of the Nazis' claims about Jews were indeed true (which, of course, was not the case), their anti-Semitism would still be (and was) pathological, since it represses the true reason the Nazis required anti-Semitism, which was to sustain their ideological position. Exactly the same holds for the claim that the Greeks are lazy: even if this were the case, the accusation would be false, because it obfuscates the complex global economic mechanisms that drove Germany, France and others to finance the "lazy" Greeks.

say, or a homeless person—they blow the whistle, and a special guard comes running to brutalize the intruders... What seems like a cheap Hollywood fiction is a reality in today's Greece. Members of the Fascist Golden Dawn movement are distributing whistles on the streets of Athens—when someone sees a suspicious foreigner, he is invited to blow the whistle, and the Golden Dawn special guards patrolling the streets will arrive to check out the suspect. This is how one defends Europe in the Spring of 2012. These anti-immigrant vigilantes are not the principal danger, however; they are merely collateral damage accompanying the true threat—the politics of austerity that has brought Greece to such a predicament.

Critics of our institutional democracy often complain that as a rule elections do not offer a true choice. For the most part what we get is a choice between a center-right and a center-left party whose programs are virtually indistinguishable. At the time of writing, the Greek elections scheduled for June 17, 2012 offer a real choice: between the establishment (New Democracy and Pasok) on the one side and Syriza on the other. And, as is usually the case, such moments of real choice throw the establishment into panic, driving them to conjure up images of social chaos, poverty, and violence if the electorate make the wrong choice. The mere possibility of a Syriza victory has sent ripples of fear through markets around the world, and, again as is usual in such cases, ideological prosopopoeia is having a heyday: markets begin to talk like a living person, expressing their "worry" at what will happen if the elections fail to produce a government with a mandate to continue the EU-IMF program of fiscal austerity and structural reform. But the ordinary people of Greece have no time to worry about such prospects; they have enough to deal with in the present, in which their lives are becoming miserable to an extent unseen in Europe in recent decades. Such predictions, of course, often become self-fulfilling prophecies, causing panic and thus bringing about the very disaster they warn of.

In his *Notes Towards a Definition of Culture*, the great conservative T. S. Eliot remarked that there are moments when the only choice is that between heresy and non-belief, that the only way to keep a religion alive is sometimes to effect a sectarian split from its corpse. This is our position today with regard to Europe. Only a new "heresy" (represented at this moment by Syriza) can save what is worth saving in the European legacy: democracy, trust in the people, egalitarian solidarity… The Europe that will win if Syriza is outmaneuvered is a "Europe with Asian values" (which, of course, has nothing to do with Asia, and everything to do with the clear and present danger of contemporary capitalism's tendency to suspend democracy).

Greece is thus Europe's singular universality: the nodal point at which the historical tendency that shapes its present appears at its purest. This is why—to paraphrase the finale of Wagner's *Parsifal*—we should redeem the redeemer. We should not only save Greece from its saviors—the European consortium testing out "austerity measures" in Dr. Mengele-like fashion—but also save Europe itself from its saviors: the neoliberals promoting the bitter medicine of austerity and the anti-immigrant populists. There is, however, something wrong with this idea: the fact it is exactly the response of the archetypal European left-liberal moron—preferably a socially aware cultural intellectual—on the question of Europe today. As a politically correct anti-racist, he will insist that, of course, he rejects anti-immigrant populism: the danger comes from within, not from Islam. The two main threats to Europe, he says, are this very populism and neoliberal economics. Against this double threat, we must resuscitate social solidarity, multicultural tolerance, the material conditions for cultural development, etcetera. But how is this to be done? The main, moronic idea here involves a return to the authentic Welfare State: we need a new political party that will return to the good old principles abandoned under neoliberal pressure; we need to regulate the banks and control financial excesses, guarantee free universal health care and education, and so on. What is wrong with this? Everything. Such an approach is *stricto sensu* idealist, that is, it opposes its own idealized ideological supplement to the existing deadlock. Recall what Marx wrote about Plato's *Republic*: the problem is not that it is "too utopian," but, on the contrary, that it remains the ideal image of the existing politico-economic order. Mutatis mutandis, we should read the ongoing dismantling of the Welfare State not as the betrayal of a noble idea, but as a failure that retroactively enables us to discern a fatal flaw of the very notion of the Welfare State. The lesson is that if we want to save the emancipatory kernel of the notion, we will have to change the terrain and rethink its most basic implications (such as the long-term viability of a "social market economy," that is, of a socially responsible capitalism).

Today, we are bombarded with a multitude of attempts to human-ize capitalism, from eco-capitalism to Basic Income capitalism. The reasoning behind these attempts goes as follows: Historical experience has demonstrated that capitalism is by far the best way to generate wealth; at the same time, it must be admitted that left to itself the process of capitalist reproduction entails exploitation, the destruc-tion of natural resources, mass suffering, injustice, wars, etcetera. Our aim should thus be to maintain the basic capitalist matrix of profit-oriented reproduction, but to steer and regulate it so that it serves the larger goals of global welfare and justice. Consequently, we should leave the capitalist beast to its own proper functioning, accepting that markets have their own demands that should be respected, that any direct disturbance of market mechanisms will lead to catastrophe—all we can hope to do is tame the beast… However, all these attempts, well intended as they often are in their endeavor to unite pragmatic realism and a principled commitment to justice, sooner or later encounter the *Real* of the antagonism between the two dimensions: the capitalist beast again and again escapes the benevolent social reg-ulation. At some point, we will thus be compelled to ask the fateful question: is playing with the capitalist beast really the only imaginable game in town? What if, productive as capitalism is, the price we have to pay for its continuous functioning simply has become too high? If we avoid this question and continue to humanize capitalism, we will only contribute to the process we are trying to reverse. Signs of this process abound everywhere, including in the rise of Wal-Mart as the representation of a new form of consumerism targeting the lower classes:

> Unlike the first large corporations that created wholly new sectors by means of some invention (e.g. Edison with the light bulb, Microsoft with its Windows software, Sony with the Walkman, or Apple with the iPod/iPhone/iTunes package), or other companies that focused on building a particular brand (e.g. Coca-Cola or Marlboro), Wal-Mart did something no one had ever thought of before. It packaged a new Ideology of Cheapness into a brand that was meant to appeal to the financially stressed American working and lower-middle classes. In conjunction with its fierce proscription of trades unions, it became a bulwark of keeping prices low and of extending to its long suffering working-class customers a sense of satisfaction for having shared in

the exploitation of the (mostly foreign) producers of the goods in their shopping basket.[7]

But the key feature is that the ongoing crisis is not about reckless spending, greed, ineffectual bank regulation, etcetera. An economic cycle is coming to an end, a cycle that began in the early 1970s, when what Varoufakis calls the "Global Minotaur" was born—the monstrous engine that ran the world economy from the early 1980s to 2008.[8] The late 1960s and the early 1970s were not just the era of the oil crisis and stagflation; Nixon's decision to abandon the gold standard for the US dollar was the sign of a much more radical shift in the basic functioning of the capitalist system. By the end of the 1960s, the US economy was no longer able to continue recycling its surpluses in Europe and Asia: its surpluses had turned into deficits. In 1971, the US government responded to this decline with an audacious strategic move. Instead of tackling the nation's burgeoning deficits, it decided to do the opposite, to *boost deficits*. And who would pay for them? The rest of the world! How? By means of a permanent transfer of capital that rushed ceaselessly across the two great oceans to finance America's deficits. The latter thus started to operate

like a giant vacuum cleaner, absorbing other people's surplus goods and capital. While that "arrangement" was the embodiment of the grossest imbalance imaginable at a planetary scale … nonetheless, it did give rise to something resembling global balance; an international system of rapidly accelerating asymmetrical financial and trade flows capable of putting on a semblance of stability and steady growth … Powered by these deficits, the world's leading surplus economies (e.g. Germany, Japan and, later, China) kept churning out the goods while America absorbed them. Almost 70 percent of the profits made globally by these countries were then transferred back to the United States, in the form of capital flows to Wall Street. And what did Wall Street do with it? It turned these capital inflows into direct investments, shares, new financial instruments, new and old forms of loans, etc.[9]

7   "The Global Minotaur: An Interview with Yanis Varoufakis," available at nakedcapitalism.com.
8   See Yanis Varoufakis, *The Global Minotaur*, London: Zed Books 2011.
9   "The Global Minotaur: An Interview with Yanis Varoufakis, naked capitalism.com."

Although Emmanuel Todd's vision of today's global order is clearly one-sided, it is difficult to deny its moment of truth: that the US is an empire in decline.[10] Its growing negative trade balance demonstrates that it is an unproductive predator. It has to suck up a daily influx of one billion dollars from other nations to pay for its consumption and is, as such, the universal Keynesian consumer that keeps the world economy running. (So much for the anti-Keynesian economic ideology that seems to predominate today!) This influx, which is effectively like the tithe paid to Rome in antiquity (or the gifts sacrificed to the Minotaur by the Ancient Greeks), relies on a complex economic mechanism: the US is "trusted" as the safe and stable center, so that all the others, from the oil-producing Arab countries to Western Europe and Japan, and now even the Chinese, invest their surplus profits in the US. Since this trust is primarily ideological and military, not economic, the problem for the US is how to justify its imperial role—it needs a permanent state of war, thus the "war on terror," offering itself as the universal protector of all other "normal" (not "rogue") states. The entire globe thus tends to function as a universal Sparta with its three classes, now emerging as the First, Second, and Third worlds: (1) the US as the military-political-ideological power; (2) Europe and parts of Asia and Latin America as the industrial-manufacturing regions (crucial here are Germany and Japan, the world's leading exporters, plus rising China); (3) the undeveloped rest, today's helots. In other words, global capitalism has brought about a new general trend towards oligarchy, masked as the celebration of the "diversity of cultures": equality and universalism are increasingly disappearing as genuine political principles. Even before it has fully established itself, however, this neo-Spartan world system is breaking down. In contrast to the situation in 1945, the world does not need the US; it is the US that needs the rest of the world.

Against the background of this gigantic shadow, the European struggles—German leaders furious with Greece and reluctant to throw billions into a black hole; Greek leaders pathetically insisting on their sovereignty and comparing the pressure from Brussels to the German occupation during World War II—cannot but appear petty and ridiculous.

---

10   See Emmanuel Todd, *After the Empire*, London: Constable 2004.

CHAPTER THREE

The "Dream-Work" of Political Representation

In his analyses of the French Revolution of 1848 and its aftermath (in *The Eighteenth Brumaire* and *Class Struggles in France*), Marx "complicated" in a properly dialectical way the logic of social representation (political agents representing economic classes and forces), going much further than the usual conception of these "complications," according to which political representation never directly mirrors social structure. (A single political agent can represent different social groups; a class can renounce its direct representation and leave to another class the task of securing the politico-juridical conditions of its rule, as the English capitalist class did by leaving the exercise of political power to the aristocracy, and so on.) Marx's analyses point towards what, more than a century later, Lacan articulated as the "logic of the signifier." There are four principal versions of Marx's "complication"—let us begin with his analysis of the Party of Order, which took power when the 1848 revolutionary élan in France had dwindled. The secret of its existence was

the coalition of Orléanists and Legitimists into one party, disclosed. The bourgeois class fell apart into two big factions which alternately—the big landed proprietors under the restored monarchy and the finance aristocracy and the industrial bourgeoisie under the July Monarchy—had maintained a monopoly of power. Bourbon was the royal name for the predominant influence of the interests of the one faction, Orléans the royal name for the predominant influence of the interests of the other faction—the nameless realm of the republic was the only one in which both factions could maintain with equal power the common class interest without giving up their mutual rivalry.[1]

This, then, is the first complication: when we are dealing with two or more socio-economic groups, their common interest can only be represented in the guise of the *negation of their shared premise*—the common denominator of the two royalist factions is not royalism, but republicanism. And, in the same way today, the only political agent that consequently represents the collective interests of Capital as such, in its universality, above its particular factions, is "Third Way" Social Democracy (which is why Wall Street supports Obama), and, in contemporary China, it is the Communist Party. In *The Eighteenth Brumaire*, Marx goes on to extend this logic to the whole of society, as is clear from his acerbic description of the "Society of December 10," Napoleon III's private army of thugs:

> Alongside decayed *roués* with dubious means of subsistence and of dubious origin, alongside ruined and adventurous offshoots of the bourgeoisie, were vagabonds, discharged soldiers, discharged jailbirds, escaped galley slaves, swindlers, mountebanks, *lazzaroni*, pickpockets, tricksters, gamblers, *maquereaux*, brothel keepers, porters, literati, organ grinders, ragpickers, knife grinders, tinkers, beggars—in short, the whole indefinite, disintegrated mass, thrown hither and thither, which the French call *la bohème*; from this kindred element Bonaparte formed the core of the Society of December 10 ... This Bonaparte, who constitutes himself chief of the *lumpen* proletariat, who here alone rediscovers in mass form the interests which he personally pursues, who recognizes in this scum, offal, refuse of all classes the only class upon which he can base himself unconditionally, is the real Bonaparte, the Bonaparte *sans phrase*.[2]

The logic of the Party of Order is here brought to its radical conclusion: *the only common denominator of all classes is the excremental excess, the refuse/remainder of all classes.* In other words, insofar as Napoleon III perceived himself as standing above class interests, for

---

1   Karl Marx and Friedrich Engels, *Selected Works*, Volume 1, Moscow: Progress Publishers 1969, p. 83.
2   Karl Marx and Friedrich Engels, *Collected Works*, Volume 2, Moscow: Progress Publishers 1975, p. 148.

the reconciliation of all classes, his immediate class base can only be the excremental remainder of all classes, the rejected non-class of each class. So, in a properly Hegelian dialectical reversal, it is precisely the non-representable excess of society, the scum, the plebs, which is by definition left out in any organic system of social representation, which becomes the medium of universal representation. And it is this support in the "socially abject" that enables Napoleon to run around, constantly shifting his position, representing in turn each class against all others:

> The people are to be given employment: initiation of public works. But the public works increase the people's tax obligations: hence reduction of taxes by an attack on the *rentiers*, by conversion of the 5 percent bonds into 4½ percent. But the middle class must again receive a sweetening: hence a doubling of the wine tax for the people, who buy wine retail, and a halving of the wine tax for the middle class, which drinks it wholesale; dissolution of the actual workers' associations, but promises of miraculous future associations. The peasants are to be helped: mortgage banks which hasten their indebtedness and accelerate the concentration of property. But these banks are to be used to make money out of the confiscated estates of the House of Orleans; no capitalist wants to agree to this condition, which is not in the decree, and the mortgage bank remains a mere decree, etc., etc.
>
> Bonaparte would like to appear as the patriarchal benefactor of all classes. But he cannot give to one without taking from another. Just as it was said of the Duke de Guise in the time of the *Fronde* that he was the most obliging man in France because he gave all his estates to his followers, with feudal obligations to him, so Bonaparte would like to be the most obliging man in France and turn all the property and all the labor of France into a personal obligation to himself. He would like to steal all of France in order to make a present of it to France.[3]

We encounter here the deadlock of the All: if all (classes) are to be represented, then the structure has to be like that of *le jeu du furet* ("ferret game"), in which players form a circle around one person and quickly pass the "ferret" behind their backs; the player in the center then has to guess who holds the ferret—if he guesses right, he changes places

---

3   Karl Marx, "The Eighteenth Brumaire of Louis Bonaparte" (1852), *Surveys From Exile*, ed. David Fernbach, Harmondsworth: Penguin 1973, pp 246–7.

with the one who had the ferret. (In the English version, the players shout, "Button, button, who's got the button?") However, this is not all. In order for the system to function, that is, in order for Napoleon to stand above all classes and not to act as a direct representative of any class, it is not enough for him to locate the direct base of his regime in the refuse or remainder of all classes. He also has to act as the representative of one particular class, of that class which, precisely, is not constituted to act as a united agent demanding active representation. This class of people who cannot represent themselves and can thus only be represented is, of course, the class of small-holding peasants:

> The small-holding peasants form an enormous mass whose members live in similar conditions but without entering into manifold relations with each other. Their mode of production isolates them from one another instead of bringing them into mutual intercourse ... They are therefore incapable of asserting their class interest in their own name, whether through a parliament or a convention. They cannot represent themselves, they must be represented. Their representative must at the same time appear as their master, as an authority over them, an unlimited governmental power which protects them from the other classes and sends them rain and sunshine from above. The political influence of the small-holding peasants, therefore, finds its final expression in the executive power which subordinates society to itself.[4]

Only these features together form the paradoxical structure of populist-Bonapartist representation: *standing above* all classes; *shifting between* them; direct reliance on the *abject remainder of all classes*; plus the ultimate reference to the class of those who are *unable to act as a collective agent demanding political representation*.[5] What these paradoxes point towards is the impossibility of pure representation (recall the stupidity of Rick Santorum who in early 2012 said that, in contrast to Occupy Wall Street, which claims to stand for the 99 percent, he represents the entire 100 percent). As Lacan would

---

4   Ibid.
5   It is not difficult to discern in this trinity the Lacanian triad of the ISR: the small farmers as the Imaginary base of Napoleon III's regime; the Symbolic ferret game of jumping from one to another (sub)class; the Real of the scum of all classes.

have put it, the class antagonism renders such a total representation materially impossible: class antagonism means that there is no neutral All of a society—every "All" secretly privileges a certain class.

Recall the axiom followed by the great majority of contemporary "specialists" and politicians: we are told again and again that we live in critical times of deficit and debt and will all have to share the burden and accept a lower standard of living—*all, that is, with the exception of the (very) rich.* The idea of taxing them more is an absolute taboo: if we do this, so we are told, the rich will lose any incentive to invest and thereby create new jobs, and we will all suffer the consequences. The only way out of these hard times is for the poor to get poorer and the rich to get richer. And if the rich look to be in danger of losing some of their wealth, society must help them out. The predominant view of the financial crisis (that it was caused by excessive state borrowing and spending) is blatantly in conflict with the fact that, from Iceland to the US, the ultimate responsibility for it lies with the big private banks—in order to prevent their collapse, the state had to intervene with enormous sums of taxpayers' money.

The standard way of disavowing an antagonism and presenting one's own position as the representation of the All is to project the cause of the antagonism onto a foreign intruder who stands for the threat to society as such, for the anti-social element, for its excremental excess. This is why anti-Semitism is not just one among many ideologies; it is ideology as such, *kat'exohen*. It embodies the zero-level (or the pure form) of ideology, establishing its elementary coordinates: the social antagonism ("class struggle") is mystified or displaced so that its cause can be projected onto the external intruder. Lacan's formula "1 + 1 + a" is best exemplified by the class struggle: the two classes plus the excess of the "Jew," the *objet a*, the supplement to the antagonistic couple. The function of this supplementary element is double. It involves a fetishistic disavowal of class antagonism, and yet, precisely as such, it stands for this antagonism, forever preventing "class peace." In other words, were there only the two classes, 1 + 1, without the supplement, then we would not have "pure" class antagonism but, on the contrary, class peace: the two classes complementing each other in a harmonious Whole. The paradox is thus that the very element that blurs or displaces the "purity" of the class struggle also serves as its motivating force. Critics of Marxism who insist that there are never just two classes opposed in social life thus miss the point: *it is precisely because there are never only two opposed classes that there is class struggle.*

This brings us to the changes in the "Napoleon III dispositif" that occurred in the twentieth century. First, the specific role of the "Jew" (or its structural equivalent) as the foreign intruder who poses a threat to the social body was not yet fully developed, and one can easily show that foreign immigrants are today's Jews, the main target of the new populism.

Second, today's small farmers are the notorious middle class. The ambiguity of the middle class, this contradiction embodied (as Marx put it apropos Proudhon), is best exemplified by the way it relates to politics: On the one hand, the middle class is against politicization—it just wants to maintain its way of life, to be left to work and live in peace, which is why it tends to support authoritarian coups that promise to put an end to the crazy political mobilization of society, so that everybody can return to his or her rightful place. On the other hand, members of the middle class—now in the guise of a threatened patriotic hard-working moral majority—are the main instigators of grassroots right-wing populist movements, from Le Pen in France and Geert Wilders in the Netherlands to the Tea Party movement in the US.

Finally, as part of the global shift from the discourse of the Master to the discourse of the University, a new figure has emerged—that of the (technocratic, financial) *expert* who is allegedly able to rule (or rather, "administer") in a neutral post-ideological way, without representing any specific interests.

But where in all this is the usual suspect identified by the orthodox Marxist analysis of fascism—the big capital (corporations like Krupp, etcetera) that "really stood behind Hitler"? (The orthodox Marxist *doxa* violently rejected the theory of middle-class support for Hitler.) Orthodox Marxism is correct here, but for the wrong reasons: big capital *is* the ultimate reference, the "absent cause," but it exerts its causality precisely through a series of displacements—or, to quote Kojin Karatani's precise homology with the Freudian logic of dreams: "What Marx emphasizes [in his *Eighteenth Brumaire*] is not the 'dream-thoughts'—in other words, the actual relationships of class interest—but rather the 'dream-work,' in other words, the ways in which class unconsciousness is condensed and displaced."[6]

Perhaps, however, we should invert Karatani's formula: are not "dream-thoughts" rather the contents/interests represented in multiple ways through the mechanisms described by Marx (small farmers, *lumpenproletariat*, etcetera), and is not the "unconscious wish," the Real of the "absent Cause" overdetermining this game of multiple representations, the interest of big Capital? The Real is simultaneously the Thing to which direct access is not possible *and* the obstacle that prevents this direct access; the Thing that eludes our grasp *and* the distorting screen that makes us miss the Thing. More precisely, the Real is ultimately the very shift of perspective from the first to the second standpoint: the Lacanian Real is not only distorted, but *the very principle of the distortion* of reality. This *dispositif* is strictly homologous to Freud's interpretation of dreams: for Freud too, the unconscious desire in a dream is not simply its core, which never appears directly, distorted by its translation into the manifest dream-text, but is the very principle of this distortion. This is also how, for Deleuze, in a strict conceptual homology, the economic plays its role of determining the social structure "in the last instance". Here the economic is never directly present as an actual causal agent, its presence is purely virtual, it is the social "pseudo-cause," but, precisely as such, absolute, non-relational, the absent cause, something that is never "at its own place": "that is why 'the economic' is never given properly speaking, but rather designates a differential virtuality to be interpreted, always covered over by its forms of actualization."[7] It is the absent X that circulates between the multiple series of the social field (economic, political, ideological, legal...), *distributing them in their specific articulations.* We should thus insist on the radical difference between the economic as this virtual X, the absolute point of reference of the social field, and the economic in its actuality, as one element ("sub-system") of the actual social totality: when they encounter each other—or, to put it in Hegelese, when the virtual economic encounters itself in its "oppositional determination," in the

6   Kojin Karatani, *History and Repetition*, New York: Columbia University Press 2011, p. 12.

7   Gilles Deleuze, *Difference and Repetition*, New York: Columbia University Press 1995, p. 186.

guise of its actual counterpart—this identity coincides with absolute (self-)contradiction.

As Lacan put it in his Seminar XI, "*il n'y a de cause que de ce qui cloche*"—there is no cause but a cause of something that stumbles/slips/falters[8]—a thesis whose clearly paradoxical character is explained when one takes into account the opposition between cause and causality. For Lacan, they are in no sense the same thing, since a "cause," in the strict sense of the term, is precisely something that intervenes at those points where the network of causality (the chain of cause and effect) falters, when there is a break, a gap, in the causal chain. In this sense, a cause is for Lacan by definition a distant cause (an "absent cause," as the jargon of the happy "structuralism" of the 1960s and 1970s used to have it)—it acts in the interstices of the direct causal network. What Lacan has in mind here specifically is the working of the unconscious. Imagine an ordinary slip of the tongue: at a chemistry conference, for example, someone gives a speech about, say, the exchange of fluids; all of a sudden, he stumbles and makes a slip, blurting out something about the passage of sperm in sexual intercourse—an "attractor" from what Freud called "an Other Scene" has intervened like a force of gravity, exerting its invisible influence from a distance, curving the space of the speech-flow, introducing a gap into it. And perhaps this is also how we should understand the infamous Marxist formula of "determination in the last instance": the overdetermining instance of "economy" is also a distant cause, never direct, it intervenes in the gaps of direct social causality.

How, then, does the "determining role of economy" function, if it is not the ultimate referent of the social field? Imagine a political struggle fought out in the terms of popular musical culture, as was the case in some post-socialist Eastern European countries in which the tension between pseudo-folk and rock functioned as a displacement of the tension between the nationalist-conservative right and the liberal left. To put it in old-fashioned terms: a popular-cultural struggle "expressed" (provided the terms in which) a political struggle (was fought out). (As today in the US, with country music predominantly conservative and rock predominantly left-liberal.) Following Freud, it is not enough to say that the struggle taking place in popular

8   See Chapter 1 of Jacques Lacan, *The Four Fundamental Concepts of Psycho-Analysis*, Harmondsworth: Penguin 1979.

music was here only a secondary expression, a symptom, an encoded translation, of the political struggle, which was what the whole thing "was really about." Both struggles have a substance of their own: the cultural is not just a secondary phenomenon, a battlefield of shadows to be "deciphered" for its political connotations (which, as a rule, are obvious enough).

The "determining role of economy" thus does not mean that, in this case, what all the fuss "was really about" was the economic struggle, with the economic functioning as a hidden meta-Essence "expressing" itself at a distance twice removed in cultural struggle (the economy determines politics which in turn determines culture ...). On the contrary, the economic inscribes itself in the course of the very translation or transposition of the political struggle into the popular-cultural struggle, a transposition that is never direct, but always displaced, asymmetrical. The "class" connotation, as it is encoded in cultural "ways of life," can often invert the explicit political connotation. Recall how, in the famous presidential TV debate in 1959, generally held to be responsible for Nixon's defeat, it was the progressive Kennedy who was perceived as an upper-class patrician, while the rightist Nixon appeared as his lower-class opponent. This, of course, does not mean that the second opposition simply belies the first, that the second stands for the "truth" obfuscated by the first—that is, that Kennedy who, in his public statements, presented himself as Nixon's progressive, liberal opponent, signaled by his lifestyle that he was *really* an upper-class patrician. But it does mean that the displacement bears witness to the limitations of Kennedy's progressivism, since it does point towards the contradictory nature of his ideologico-political position.[9] And it is here that the determining instance of the "economy" operates: the economy is the absent cause that accounts for the displacement in representation, for the asymmetry (reversal, in this case) between the two series, the couple "progressive/conservative politics" and the couple "upper/middle class."

"Politics" is thus a name for *the distance of the economy from itself.* Its space is opened up by the gap that separates the economy as the absent Cause from the economy in its "oppositional determination," as

---

9   The same reversal continues today, when the opposition of liberal-left feminists and conservative populists is also perceived as an opposition between upper-middle-class feminists or multiculturalists and lower-class rednecks.

one of the elements of the social totality: there is politics *because* the economy is "non-All," because the economy is an "impotent," impassive, pseudo-cause. The economic is thus here doubly inscribed in the precise sense that defines the Lacanian Real: it is simultaneously the hard core "expressed" in other struggles through displacements and other forms of distortion, and the very structuring principle of these distortions.

In its long and twisted history, the Marxist social hermeneutic relied on two logics that, although often confounded under the ambiguous shared title of "economic class struggle," are quite distinct from each other. On the one hand, there is the (in)famous "economic interpretation of history": all struggles—artistic, ideological, political—are ultimately conditioned by the economic ("class") struggle, wherein lies their secret meaning waiting to be deciphered. On the other hand, "everything is political"; in other words, the Marxist view of history is thoroughly politicized, there are no social, ideological, cultural, or other phenomena that are not "contaminated" by the essential political struggle, and this goes even for the economy: the illusion of "trade-unionism" is precisely that the workers' struggle can be depoliticized, reduced to a purely economic negotiation for better working conditions, wages and so on. However, these two "contaminations"—the economic determines everything "in the last instance" and "everything is political"—do not obey the same logic. The economic without the ex-timate political core ("class struggle") would be a positive social matrix of development, as it is in the (pseudo-)Marxist evolutionary-historicist notion of development. On the other hand, "pure" politics, "decontaminated" from the economic, is no less ideological: vulgar economism and ideologico-political idealism are two sides of the same coin. The structure is here that of an inward loop: "class struggle" is politics in the very heart of the economic. Or, to put it paradoxically: one can reduce all political, juridical, cultural content to an "economic base," "deciphering" it as its "expression"—all, that is, *except* class struggle, which is politics in the economy itself.[10] Class struggle is thus

10   Mutatis mutandis, the same holds for psychoanalysis: all dreams have a sexual content *except* explicitly sexual dreams—why? Because the sexualization of a content is formal, the principle of its distortion: through repetition, oblique approach, etcetera, every topic—inclusive of sexuality itself—is sexualized. The ultimate properly Freudian lesson is that the explosion of human symbolic capacities does not merely expand the metaphoric scope of sexuality

a unique mediating term that, while mooring politics in the economy (all politics is "ultimately" an expression of class struggle), simultaneously stands for the irreducible political moment at the very heart of the economic.

What lies at the root of these paradoxes is the constitutive excess of representation over the represented that seems to escape Marx. In other words, in spite of his many perspicuous analyses (like those in *The Eighteenth Brumaire*), Marx ultimately reduced the state to an epiphenomenon of the "economic base"; as such, the state is determined by the logic of representation: which class does the state represent? The paradox here is that it was this neglect of the proper weight of the state machinery that gave birth to the Stalinist state, to what one is quite justified in calling "state socialism." Lenin, after the end of the civil war, which left Russia devastated and practically without a working class (most workers having been wiped out fighting the counter-revolution), was already bothered by the problem of state representation: what now was the "class base" of the Soviet state? Whom did it represent insofar as it clamed to be a working-class state, when the working class had been reduced to a tiny minority? What Lenin forgot to include in the series of possible candidates for this role was *the state (apparatus) itself*, a mighty machine of millions that held all the economico-political power. As in the joke quoted by Lacan—"I have three brothers, Paul, Ernest and myself"—the Soviet state represented three classes: poor farmers, workers, *and itself*. Or, to put it in István Mészáros's terms, Lenin forgot to take into account the role of the state *within* the "economic base," as its key factor. Far from preventing the growth of a tyrannical state free from any mechanism of social control, this neglect opened up the space for the state's untrammeled

---

(activities that are in themselves thoroughly asexual can become "sexualized," everything can be "eroticized"), but that, much more importantly, this explosion *sexualizes sexuality itself*: the specific quality of human sexuality has nothing to do with the immediate, rather stupid, reality of copulation, including the preparatory mating rituals. It is only when animal coupling gets caught up in the self-referential vicious circle of the drive, in the protracted repetition of its failure to reach the impossible Thing, that we get what we call sexuality, that sexual activity itself is sexualized. In other words, the fact that sexuality can spill over and function as the metaphoric content of every (other) human activity is not a sign of its power but, on the contrary, a sign of its impotence, its failure, its inherent blockage.

power: only if we admit that the state represents not only social classes external to itself but also itself are we led to raise the question of who will contain the power of the state.

Thomas Frank has aptly described the paradox of populist conservatism in the US today, the basic premise of which is the gap between economic interests and "moral" questions.[11] In other words, the economic class opposition (poor farmers and blue-collar workers versus lawyers, bankers, large companies) is transposed or coded into the opposition between honest hard-working Christian Americans and the decadent liberals who drink lattes and drive foreign cars, advocate abortion and homosexuality, mock patriotic sacrifice and the simple provincial way of life, and so on. The enemy is thus perceived as the "liberal" who, through federal state intervention (from school-busing to prescribing that Darwinian evolution and perverse sexual practices be taught in class), wants to undermine the authentic American way of life. The populist conservatives' central economic proposition is therefore to get rid of the strong state that taxes the hard-working population in order to finance its regulatory interventions—their minimal program is thus "fewer taxes, less regulation."

From the standard perspective of the rational pursuit of self-interest, the inconsistency of this ideological stance is obvious: the populist conservatives are literally *voting themselves into economic ruin*. Less taxation and deregulation means more freedom for the big companies that are driving the impoverished farmers out of business; less state intervention means less federal help for small farmers; and so on down the line. In the eyes of the American evangelical populists, the state stands for an alien power and, together with the UN, is an agent of the Antichrist. It is taking away the liberty of the Christian believer, relieving him of the moral responsibility of stewardship, and thus undermines the individualistic morality that makes each of us the architect of our own salvation. But how is this compatible with the unprecedented explosion of the state apparatuses under George W. Bush? No wonder large corporations are delighted at such evangelical attacks on the state, when the state tries to regulate media mergers, put restrictions on energy companies, strengthen air pollution regulations, protect wildlife and limit logging in the national parks, etcetera.

---

11   See Thomas Frank, *What's the Matter with Kansas? How Conservatives Won the Heart of America*, New York: Metropolitan Books 2004.

It is the ultimate irony of history that radical individualism serves as an ideological justification for the unconstrained power of what the vast majority experience as an anonymous force that, without any democratic public control, regulates their lives.

As to the ideological aspect of their struggle, it is glaringly obvious that the populists are fighting a war that simply *cannot be won*: if Republicans were to ban abortion, if they were to prohibit the teaching of evolution, if they were to impose censorship on Hollywood and mass culture, this would entail not only their immediate ideological defeat, but also a large-scale economic depression in the US. The outcome is thus a debilitating symbiosis: although the "ruling class" disagrees with the populist moral agenda, it tolerates the "moral war" as a means of keeping the lower classes in check, allowing them to articulate their fury without disturbing vested economic interests. What this means is that the *culture war is a class war* in a displaced mode—pace those who claim that we live in a post-class society.

This, however, makes the enigma only more impenetrable: how is this displacement *possible*? "Stupidity" and "ideological manipulation" are not the answer; for it is clearly inadequate to say the lower classes have been so brainwashed by ideology they are unable to identify their true interests. If nothing else, we should recall how, years ago, Kansas was a hotbed of *progressive* populism in the US—and people have certainly not become more stupid over the last few decades. Nor would a direct psychoanalytic explanation in the old Wilhelm Reich style (people's libidinal investments compel them to act against their rational interests) be adequate: it confronts the libidinal economy and the economy proper too directly, failing to grasp their mediation. The solution proposed by Ernesto Laclau is also ultimately unsatisfying: there is no "natural" link between a given socio-economic position and the ideology attached to it, so that it is meaningless to speak of "deception" and "false consciousness," as if there were a standard of "appropriate" ideological awareness inscribed into the "objective" socio-economic situation itself; every ideological edifice is the outcome of a hegemonic struggle to establish or impose a chain of equivalences, a struggle whose outcome is thoroughly contingent, not guaranteed by any external reference such as the "objective socio-economic position." In such a general answer, the enigma simply disappears.

The first thing to note here is that it takes two to fight a culture war: culture is also the dominant ideological topic of the "enlightened" liberals whose politics is focused on the fight against sexism, racism, and fundamentalism, and for multicultural tolerance. The key question is thus: why has "culture" emerged as our central life-world category? With regard to religion, we no longer "really believe," we simply follow (some of the) religious rituals and mores as part of our respect for the "lifestyle" of the community to which we belong (non-believing Jews obeying kosher rules "out of respect for tradition," etcetera). "I don't really believe in it, it's just part of my culture" seems to be the predominant mode of the disavowed or displaced belief characteristic of our times. Perhaps, then, the "non-fundamentalist" notion of "culture" as distinguished from "real" religion, art, and so on, *is* in its very core the name for the field of disowned or impersonal beliefs—"culture" as the name for all those things we practice without really believing in them, without "taking them seriously."

The second thing to note is how, while professing their solidarity with the poor, liberals encode their culture war with an opposed class message. More often than not, their fight for multicultural tolerance and women's rights marks the counter-position to the alleged intolerance, fundamentalism, and patriarchal sexism of the "lower classes." One way to unravel this confusion is to focus on the mediating terms whose function is to obfuscate the true lines of division. The way the term "modernization" has been used in the recent ideological offensive is exemplary here: first, an abstract opposition is constructed between "modernizers" (those who endorse global capitalism in all its aspects, from the economic to the cultural) and "traditionalists" (those who resist globalization). Into this category of those-who-resist is then thrown everyone from traditional conservatives and populists to the "Old Left" (those who continue to advocate the welfare state, trade unions, and so on). This categorization obviously does capture an aspect of social reality. Recall the coalition between the Church and trade unions in Germany in early 2003, which prevented the legalization of Sunday opening for shops. However, it is not enough to say that this "cultural difference" traverses the entire social field, cutting across different strata and classes; it is also inadequate to say that it can be combined in different ways with other oppositions (so that we get conservative "traditional values" resisting global capitalist "modernization," or moral conservatives who fully endorse capitalist globalization). In short, it is useless to claim that this "cultural difference" is one in a series of antagonisms operative in contemporary social processes.

The failure of this opposition to function as the key to the social totality means not only that it should be articulated with other differences. It means that it is "abstract," and the wager of Marxism is that there is one antagonism (class struggle) which overdetermines all the others and which is as such the "concrete universal" of the entire field. The term "overdetermination" is here used in its precise Althusserian sense: it does not mean that class struggle is the ultimate referent and horizon of meaning of all other struggles; it means that class struggle is the structuring principle that allows us to account for the very "inconsistent" plurality of ways in which other antagonisms can be articulated into "chains of equivalences." For example, the feminist struggle can be articulated into a chain with the progressive struggle for emancipation, or it can (as it certainly often does) function as an ideological tool with which the upper-middle classes assert their superiority over the "patriarchal and intolerant" lower classes. The point is not only that the feminist struggle can be articulated in different ways with the class antagonism, but that the class antagonism is, as it were, doubly inscribed here: it is the specific constellation of the class struggle itself that explains why the feminist struggle was appropriated by the upper classes. (The same goes for racism: it is the dynamics of class struggle itself that explain why open racism is more prevalent among the lowest strata of white workers.) Class struggle is here "concrete universality" in the strict Hegelian sense: in relating to its otherness (other antagonisms), it relates to itself, it (over)determines the way it relates to other struggles.

The third thing to underline is the fundamental difference between feminist, anti-racist, anti-sexist and other such struggles and the class struggle. In the first case, the goal is to translate antagonism into difference (the peaceful coexistence of sexes, religions, ethnic groups), while the goal of the class struggle is precisely the opposite, to turn class differences into class antagonisms. The point of subtraction is to reduce the overall complex structure to its antagonistic minimal difference. What the series race-gender-class obfuscates is the different logic of the political space in the case of class: while anti-racist and anti-sexist struggles are guided by a striving for the full recognition of the other, the class struggle aims at overcoming and subduing, annihilating even, the other—even if not a direct physical annihilation, it aims at wiping out the other's socio-political role and function. In other words, while it is logical to say that anti-racism wants all races to be allowed to freely assert and to realize their cultural, political, and economic strivings, it is obviously meaningless to say that the aim of the proletarian class struggle is to allow the bourgeoisie to fully assert its identity and realize its goals. In the one case, we have a horizontal logic of the recognition of different identities, while in the other we have the logic of the struggle with an antagonist. The paradox here is that it is populist fundamentalism that retains this logic of antagonism, while the liberal left follows the logic of recognition of difference, of defusing antagonisms into coexisting differences. In their very form, conservative-populist grassroots campaigns took over the old leftist-radical stance of popular mobilization and struggle against upper-class exploitation. Insofar as, in the US two-party system, red designates Republicans and blue Democrats, and insofar as populist fundamentalists (of course) vote Republican, the old anti-Communist slogan "Better dead than red!" now acquires a new and ironic meaning—the irony residing in the unexpected continuity between the "red" attitude of the old-style leftist grassroots mobilization and the new Christian fundamentalist populism.

CHAPTER FOUR

The Return of the Evil Ethnic Thing

Back in the 1930s, Hitler offered anti-Semitism as a narrative explanation for the troubles experienced by ordinary Germans: unemployment, moral decay, social unrest—behind all this stood the Jew. Evoking the "Jewish plot" made everything clear by providing a simple cognitive map. Does not today's hatred of multiculturalism and of the immigrant threat function in a homologous way? Strange things are happening—financial crashes occur that affect our daily lives, but are experienced as totally opaque—and the rejection of multiculturalism introduces a false clarity into the situation: it is the foreign intruders who are disturbing our way of life. There is thus an interconnection between the rising tide of anti-immigrant feeling in Western countries—which reached a peak in Anders Behring Breivik's killing spree—and the financial crisis: clinging to ethnic identity serves as a protective shield against the trauma of being caught up in the vortex of non-transparent financial abstraction. The true "foreign body" that cannot be assimilated is ultimately the infernal self-propelling machine of Capital itself.

There are elements that should cause us to reflect on Breivik's ideological self-justification as well as on the reactions to his murderous act. The manifesto of this Christian "Marxist hunter" who killed more than seventy people in Norway is precisely *not* a case of a madman's rambling; it is a substantive exposition of "Europe's crisis" that serves as the (more or less) implicit justification for the growing anti-immigrant populism. Its very inconsistencies are symptomatic of the inner contradictions of this view. The first thing that stands out is how Breivik constructs his enemy, from a combination of three elements (Marxism, multiculturalism, Islamism) each of which belongs to a different political space: the Marxist radical left, multiculturalist liberalism, Islamic religious fundamentalism. The old fascist habit of attributing to the enemy mutually exclusive features (the "Bolshevik-plutocratic Jewish plot") returns here in a new guise. Even more telling is the way Breivik's self-designation shuffles the cards of radical rightist ideology. He advocates Christianity, but remains a secular agnostic: Christianity is for him merely a cultural construct to oppose Islam. He is anti-feminist and thinks women should be discouraged from pursuing higher education; but he favors a "secular" society, supports abortion rights, and declares himself pro-gay. Furthermore, Breivik combines Nazi traits (for example, his sympathy for Saga, the Swedish pro-Nazi folk singer) with a hatred of Hitler: one of his heroes is Max Manus, the leader of the Norwegian anti-Nazi resistance. Breivik is not so much racist as anti-Muslim: all his hatred is focused on the Muslim threat. And, last but not least, Breivik is anti-Semitic but pro-Israel, since the State of Israel is the first line of defense against Muslim expansionism—he even wants to see the Temple in Jerusalem rebuilt. His view is that Jews are acceptable so long as there are not too many of them—or, as he wrote in his "Manifesto": "There is no Jewish problem in Western Europe (with the exception of the UK and France) as we only have 1 million in Western Europe, whereas 800,000 out of these 1 million live in France and the UK. The US on the other hand, with more than 6 million Jews (600% more than Europe) actually has a considerable Jewish problem." Breivik thus embodies the ultimate paradox of a Zionist Nazi—how is this possible?

A key is provided by the reactions of the European right to Breivik's attack. Its mantra was that, in condemning his murderous act, we should not overlook the fact that he addressed "legitimate concerns about genuine problems"—mainstream politics is failing to address the corrosion of Europe by Islamicization and multiculturalism, or, to quote the *Jerusalem Post*, we should use the Oslo tragedy "as an opportunity to seriously reevaluate policies for immigrant integration in Norway and elsewhere."[1] (It would be nice to hear a similar appreciation of Palestinian acts of terror, something like "these acts

---

1   Editorial on "Norway's Challenge," *Jerusalem Post*, July 24, 2011.

should serve as an opportunity to reevaluate Israeli policies.") A reference to Israel is, of course, implicit in this evaluation: a "multicultural" Israel has no chance of surviving, thus apartheid is the only realistic option. The price for this properly perverse Zionist-rightist pact is that, in order to justify the claim to Palestine, one has to acknowledge retroactively a line of argument that in earlier European history had been used against the Jews: the implicit deal is "We are ready to acknowledge your intolerance towards other cultures in your midst if you acknowledge our right not to tolerate Palestinians in our midst." The tragic irony is that, over the last few centuries in Europe, the Jews themselves were the first "multiculturalists": their problem was how to survive and keep their culture intact in places where another culture was predominant.[2] At the end of this road lies an extreme possibility that should in no way be excluded a priori—that of a "historic pact" between Zionists and Muslim fundamentalists.

This is why the very designation of the Middle East negotiations as a "peace process" is in itself a mystification. The true issue is not peace, but the liberation of the Palestinians—how the Palestinians are to get back (part of) the land taken from them and establish full political autonomy. In other words, the issue is not about peace in the same way in which, say, the colonial wars in Indochina or Algiers were not about peace between France and the colonized population. The moment we accept the designation "peace process," we already endorse the position of the one in whose interest it is to have peace *under the present conditions of the occupation*.

But what if we *are* entering a new era in which this new reasoning will impose itself? What if Europe should accept the paradox that its democratic openness is based on exclusion: that there is "no freedom for the enemies of freedom," as Robespierre put it long ago? In principle, this is of course true, but it is here that one has to be very specific. In a way, Breivik was justified in his choice of target: he did not attack the foreigners themselves but those within his own community who were overly tolerant towards them. The problem is not foreigners, it

---

2   Incidentally, one should note here that in the 1930s, in direct response to Nazi anti-Semitism, Ernest Jones, the main agent of the conformist gentrification of psychoanalysis, engaged in weird reflections on the percentage of foreigners a national population can tolerate in its midst without endangering its own identity—thereby accepting the Nazi problematic.

is our own (European) identity. Although the ongoing crisis of the European Union appears as a crisis of the economy and the financial system, it is in its fundamental dimension an *ideologico-political* crisis: the failure of referenda on the EU constitutional treaty a couple of years ago gave a clear signal that voters perceived the EU as a technocratic economic union, lacking any vision capable of mobilizing people. Until the recent protests, the only ideology capable of rousing people was that premised on the need to "defend Europe" against immigration.

Recent outbursts of homophobia in the East European post-Communist states should give us pause for thought. In early 2011, thousands took part in a gay parade in Istanbul without violence or disturbance; in gay parades that took place at the same time in Serbia and Croatia (Belgrade and Split), the police were unable to protect the participants, who were ferociously attacked by thousands of violent Christian fundamentalists. *These* kinds of fundamentalists, not those in Turkey, stand for the true threat to the European legacy; so in relation to the EU basically blocking Turkey's entry into the Union, the obvious question arises: what about applying the same rules to Eastern Europe?[3]

It is crucial to locate anti-Semitism in this series, as one element alongside other forms of racism, sexism, homophobia, and so forth. In order to ground its Zionist politics, the State of Israel is here making a catastrophic mistake: it decided to downplay, if not outright ignore, so-called "old" (traditional European) anti-Semitism, focusing instead on the "new" and allegedly "progressive" anti-Semitism masked as a critique of the Zionist politics of the State of Israel. Along these lines, Bernard-Henri Lévy (in his *The Left in Dark Times*) recently claimed that the anti-Semitism of the twenty-first century will be "progressive" or not at all. Pushed to its conclusion, this thesis compels us to invert the old Marxist interpretation of anti-Semitism as a mystified/ displaced anti-capitalism (instead of blaming the capitalist system, the rage is focused on a specific ethnic group accused of corrupting the system). For Lévy and his partisans, today's anti-capitalism is a disguised form of anti-Semitism.

---

3   Not to mention the weird fact that the main force behind the anti-gay movement in Croatia is the Catholic Church, well known for numerous paedophile scandals involving priests and young boys.

This unspoken but no less effective prohibition on attacking "old-style" anti-Semitism is taking place at the very moment when it is reappearing across Europe, especially in the post-Communist countries. We can observe a similar weird alliance in the US: how can the American Christian fundamentalists, who are, as it were, by nature anti-Semitic, now passionately support the Zionist policy of the State of Israel? There is only one solution to this enigma: it is not that the US fundamentalists have changed, it is that Zionism itself, in its hatred of those Jews who do not fully identify with the politics of the State of Israel, paradoxically became anti-Semitic, for it has constructed the figure of the Jew who doubts the Zionist project along anti-Semitic lines. Israel is engaged in a Faustian pact. Fox News, the main voice of the radical right in the US and a staunch supporter of Israeli expansionism, recently had to demote Glenn Beck, its most popular host, whose comments were becoming openly anti-Semitic.[4]

The standard Zionist argument against critics of the State of Israel is that, of course, like every other state, Israel can and should be judged and eventually criticized, but that the critics misuse this justified critique of Israeli policy for anti-Semitic purposes. When the unconditional Christian fundamentalist supporters of Israel reject leftist critiques of Israeli policies, their implicit line of argument is best rendered by a wonderful cartoon published in July 2008 in the Viennese daily *Die Presse*. It shows two stocky Nazi-looking Austrians, one of them holding a newspaper and commenting to his friend: "Here you

---

4   Another figure in this series of anti-Semitic Zionists is John Hagee, the founder and National Chairman of the Christian-Zionist organization, Christians United for Israel. A leading advocate of the standard Christian-conservative agenda (Hagee sees the Kyoto Protocol as a conspiracy aimed at manipulating the US economy; in his bestselling novel *Jerusalem Countdown*, the Antichrist is the head of the European Union), Hagee has been to Israel twenty-two times and has met with every Israeli prime minister since Begin. However, despite his professed "Christian Zionist" beliefs and public support for the state of Israel, Hagee has made statements that definitely sound anti-Semitic: he has blamed the Holocaust on Jews themselves; he has stated that Hitler's persecution was a "divine plan" to lead the Jews to form the modern state of Israel; he calls liberal Jews "poisoned" and "spiritually blind"; he admits that the preemptive nuclear attack on Iran that he favours will lead to the deaths of most Jews in Israel. (Even more curiously, he claims in *Jerusalem Countdown* that Hitler was born from a lineage of "accursed, genocidally murderous half-breed Jews.")

can see again how a totally justified anti-Semitism is being misused for a cheap critique of Israel!" Such, today, are the allies of the State of Israel. Jewish critics of Israel are regularly dismissed as self-hating Jews. However, are not the real self-haters those who secretly hate the true greatness of the Jewish nation, precisely the Zionists who have allied themselves with anti-Semites? How did we end up in such a bizarre situation?

The same goes for the disappointment after 1989. To put it in terms of the *Ninotchka* joke, as the name of the Polish movement proclaims, the dissident protesters wanted freedom and democracy without the ruthless capitalist lack of solidarity, but what they got was precisely freedom and democracy without solidarity. And the same also goes for the widely shared critical reaction to the ongoing "Orbanization" of Hungary.[5] The story is well known. Due to its overwhelming majority in the Hungarian parliament, Prime Minister Viktor Orban's rightist-populist Fidesz Party has the power to amend the constitution; furthermore, it has imposed new rules that will allow it to approve legislation in as little as a day and without substantive debate. And it is using this power to its fullest extent, passing a whole series of new laws—here are the most notorious:

A law which brands the former Communist Party and its successors as "criminal organizations," thus making the Hungarian Socialist Party and its leaders collectively and individually responsible for all criminal activities of the Communist parties that existed in the past in Hungary.

A law that creates a media control body, with members appointed by the ruling party in parliament. All media outlets will be required to register with the body to operate lawfully. The panel will be able to impose fines of up to 700,000 euros on media for "unbalanced news coverage," for publishing material the panel considers "insulting" to a particular group or "the majority," or for violating "public morality." "Gross" violations can result in denial of registration. The law also removes legal protections against the disclosure of journalists' sources.

---

5   When a papal document is designated as *Urbi et Orbi* ("for the city and for the world"), it means that it is addressed not only to the City (of Rome) but to the entire Catholic world. While most critics limit themselves to *urbi*, they neglect the *orbi* dimension of current events in Hungary.

A new law on religion gives automatic recognition to only fourteen religious organizations, forcing the remaining groups (over 300 of them, including representatives of world religions such as Buddhists, Hindus, and Muslims) to go through a difficult re-registration process. The applicant organizations will have to prove at least one hundred years of international existence or twenty years of established activity in Hungary; their authenticity and theology will be evaluated by the Hungarian Academy of Sciences, the Parliament's Human Rights and Religions Committee, and finally voted on by a two-thirds majority of the Parliament.

We could go on with this list, including the change to the very name of the state: no longer the Republic of Hungary, but just Hungary, the apolitical-ethnic sacred entity. These laws were widely criticized both inside and outside Hungary as a threat to European freedoms—the former US ambassador to Hungary even ironically suggested the country would once again need Radio Free Europe. The basic paradox of these laws resides in the tension between content and form. Although they are presented (with regard to their content) as anti-totalitarian laws, that is, although their apparent target is the rump of the Communist regime, their real target is liberal freedoms—these laws are the true attack on Europe, the true threat to the European legacy. Liberals are thus in no position to secretly indulge in the smug satisfaction that someone is doing the dirty job of cleansing the scene of "totalitarian" remainders (like those conservative Germans who, although opposed to Nazism, secretly appreciated how efficiently Hitler got rid of the Jews)—the liberals are not only next in line, they are already at the front of it.

It is easy to point out the obscene absurdities of these laws—for example, in Hungary today, dissidents who fought the old regime but are now faithful to the liberal-democratic legacy are treated by the ruling party as if they were complicit with the horrors of Communism. But liberal complacency is mistaken for another reason: it remains focused on the *urbi* of Hungary, forgetting how the *orbi* of global capitalism is implicated in it. In other words, beyond the easy condemnation of Orban's rule, we have to ask why this drift of post-Communist Eastern Europe towards rightist-nationalist populism has occurred. How can somewhere like (the no longer Republic of) Hungary emerge from happy global liberal capitalism *à la* Fukuyama? Back in the 1930s, Max Horkheimer responded to facile critics of fascism by saying that those who did not want to talk (critically) about capitalism should also keep silent about fascism. Today we should say: those who do not want to talk (critically) about the neoliberal world order should also keep silent about Hungary.

Let us mention *another* new law recently endorsed by the Hungarian parliament, one which is usually taken as belonging to the same series as the other anti-democratic laws: When implemented, the new banking law will see the central bank disappear as a separate institution and give the prime minister the power to name the central bank's vice presidents. It will also increase the number of political appointees to the monetary council, which sets the country's interest rates. Does not the democratic critique of this law strike an odd note in relation to the criticisms of the other laws? In line with Marx's ironic reference to the capitalist motto as "freedom, equality *and Bentham*," do not Western liberal critics want to impose on Hungary "freedom, democracy, *and independent central banks*"?

The economic context of this last reproach is clear, of course: "independent central banks" is shorthand for compliance with the "austerity measures" imposed by the EU and the IMF. The impression thus created is that democratic rights and neoliberal economic politics are two sides of the same coin—the obvious implication being that those who oppose neoliberal economic politics are "objectively" also a threat to freedom and democracy. One should unambiguously reject this logic: not only are the two dimensions (authentic democracy and neoliberal economy) independent of one another, but, in the specific conditions of the present, authentic democratic politics expresses itself precisely in the popular opposition to "neutral," apparently apolitical, technocratic economic measures. Even at the level of state policies, the control of bank transactions often proved economically successful in controlling the destructive effect of the financial crisis. This, of course, in no way justifies the economic politics of Orban's government. The point to be made was formulated clearly by the philosopher G. M. Tamas: "If the protection of democratic institutions necessarily goes hand in hand with a continual impoverishment of the Hungarian people [as the result of the austerity measures imposed by the EU and IMF], we must not be amazed that Hungarian citizens show little enthusiasm for restoring liberal democracy."[6] In other words, you cannot have it both ways, a democratic revival *and* the neoliberal politics of austerity: the coffee of democratic revival can only be served without the cream of economic neoliberalism.

The case of Hungary thus indicates the ambiguity of anti-European sentiment. When, a decade ago, Slovenians were about to join the European Union, one of our euroskeptics offered a sarcastic paraphrase of a Marx Brothers' joke about getting a lawyer: Do we Slovenes have problems? Let us join the EU! Then we will have even more problems, but we will have the EU to take care of them! This is how, today, many Slovenes perceive the EU: it brings some help, but it also brings new problems (with its regulations and fines, its demands for finance to help Greece, etcetera). Is, then, the EU worth defending? The true question is, of course, *which* EU are we referring to?

A century ago G. K. Chesterton clearly described the fundamental deadlock of critics of religion: "Men who begin to fight the Church for the sake of freedom and humanity end by flinging away freedom and humanity if only they may fight the Church ... The secularists have not wrecked divine things; but the secularists have wrecked secular things, if that is any comfort to them." Does not the same hold for the advocates of religion themselves? How many fanatical defenders of religion started by ferociously attacking contemporary secular culture and ended up forsaking any meaningful religious experience? In a similar way, many liberal warriors are so eager to fight antidemocratic fundamentalism that they will end by flinging away freedom and democracy themselves so that they may fight terror. If the "terrorists" are ready to wreck this world for love of another, our defenders are ready to wreck their own democratic world out of hatred for the Muslim other. Some of them love human dignity so much that they are ready to legalize torture—the ultimate degradation of that dignity.

And does not the same hold also for the recent defenders of Europe against the "immigrant threat"? In their fervor to protect the Judeo-Christian legacy, the new zealots are ready to forsake the true heart of the Christian legacy: each individual has an immediate access to universality (of the Holy Spirit, or, today, of human rights and freedoms);

---

6   Heti Világgazdaság, "Let us Deal With Orbán," presseurop, January 3, 2012, available at www.presseurop.eu.

I can participate in this universal dimension directly, irrespective of my special place within the global social order. Do not Christ's "scandalous" words from Luke point in the direction of such a universality, which ignores every social hierarchy? "If anyone comes to me and does not hate his father and his mother, his wife and children, his brothers and sisters—yes even his own life—he cannot be my disciple" (Luke 14:26)? Family relations stand here for any particular ethnic or hierarchical social bond that determines our place in the global Order of Things. The "hatred" enjoined by Christ is therefore not the opposite of Christian love, but its direct expression: it is love itself that enjoins us to dissociate ourselves from the organic community into which we were born; or, as Saint Paul put it, for a Christian there are neither men nor women, neither Jews nor Greeks. No wonder that, for those fully identified with a particular way of life, the appearance of Christ was seen as either a ridiculous joke or a traumatic scandal.

But the impasse of Europe goes much deeper. The true problem is that the critics of the anti-immigrant backlash, instead of defending the precious core of the European legacy, mostly limit themselves to the endless ritual of confessing Europe's own sins, of humbly accepting the limitations of the European legacy, and of celebrating the wealth of other cultures.[7] The famous lines from William Butler Yeats's "Second

---

7 As expected, the obverse of this left celebration of the Other is often a barely concealed racism. Here is an example of such racism on the part of allegedly leftist "radicals" at its most brutal, combined with a breathtaking ignorance of facts—the author is John Pilger: "Yugoslavia was a uniquely independent and multi-ethnic, if imperfect, federation that stood as a political and economic bridge in the Cold War. This was not acceptable to the expanding European Community, especially newly united Germany, which had begun a drive east to dominate its 'natural market' in the Yugoslav provinces of Croatia and Slovenia. By the time the Europeans met at Maastricht in 1991, a secret deal had been struck; Germany recognized Croatia, and Yugoslavia was doomed. In Washington, the US ensured that the struggling Yugoslav economy was denied World Bank loans and the defunct Nato was reinvented as an enforcer." (John Pilger, "Don't Forget What Happened in Yugoslavia," *New Statesman*, August 14, 2008.) (Incidentally, Slovenia and Croatia were not "provinces," but autonomous sovereign republics whose right to secession was explicitly recognized by the federal constitution.) But Pilger then surpasses even his own standards of slander with the openly racist characterization of Kosovo as a land "which has no formal economy and is run, in effect, by criminal gangs that traffic in drugs, contraband and women"—even the standard Serb nationalist propaganda would not have put it so openly (although,

Coming" thus seem to render perfectly our present predicament: "The best lack all conviction, while the worst are full of passionate intensity." This is an excellent description of the current split between anemic liberals and impassioned fundamentalists, Muslim as well as Christian. "The best" are no longer able fully to engage, while "the worst" engage in racist, religious, sexist fanaticism. How can we break out of this deadlock?

A debate in Germany may indicate the path. On October 17, 2010, Chancellor Angela Merkel declared at a meeting of young members of her conservative Christian Democratic Union: "This multicultural approach, saying that we simply live side by side and live happily with each other, has failed. Utterly failed." The least one can say is that she was consistent, echoing an earlier debate about *Leitkultur* (the dominant culture) in which conservatives insisted that every state is based on a predominant cultural space that the members of other cultures who live in the same space should respect. But instead of playing the Beautiful Soul and bemoaning the newly emerging racist Europe such statements announce, we should turn a critical eye upon ourselves, asking to what extent our own abstract multiculturalism has contributed to this sad state of things. If all sides do not share or respect the same civility, then multiculturalism turns into legally regulated mutual ignorance or hatred. The conflict about multiculturalism *is* already a conflict about *Leitkultur*: it is not a conflict between cultures, but a conflict between different visions of how different cultures can and should coexist, about the rules and practices these cultures have to share if they are to coexist.

We should thus avoid getting caught up in the liberal game of "how much tolerance can we afford?"—should we tolerate it if "they" prevent their children from going to state schools, if "they" force their women to dress and behave in a certain way, if "they" arrange their children's marriages, if "they" brutalize gays. At this level, of course, we are never tolerant enough, or else we are always already too tolerant, neglecting

---

of course, they would have agreed with it). Such ignorance is quite common among quasi-leftists defending Yugoslavia. I still remember my amusement when, in his condemnation of the NATO bombing of Serbia, Michael Parenti gave way to outrage at the senseless attack on the Crvena Zastava car factory that, he claimed, produced no arms... I should note that, while serving in the Yugoslav Army in 1975–6, I was equipped with a Crvena Zastava machine gun!

the rights of women and so on. The only way to break out of the dead-lock is to propose and fight for a positive universalistic project that can be shared by all participants. Struggles in which "there are neither men nor women, neither Jews nor Greeks" are many, from ecology to the economy. Some months ago, a small miracle happened in the occupied West Bank: Palestinian women demonstrating against the Wall were joined by a group of Jewish lesbian women from Israel. The initial mutual mistrust was dispelled in the first confrontation with the Israeli soldiers guarding the Wall, and a sublime solidarity developed, with a traditionally dressed Palestinian woman embracing a Jewish lesbian with spiky purple hair—a living symbol of what our struggle should be.

So, perhaps, the Slovene euroskeptic missed the point with his Marx Brothers joke. Instead of wasting time on a cost-benefit analysis of our membership of the EU, we should focus on what the EU really stands for. In his later years, Freud expressed his perplexity at the question. "What does a woman want?" Today, our question is rather "What does Europe want?" Mostly, it acts as a regulator of global capitalist development; sometimes, it flirts with the conservative defense of tradition. Both these paths lead to oblivion, to Europe's marginalization. The only way out of this impasse is for Europe to resuscitate its legacy of radical and universal emancipation. The task is to move beyond the mere tolerance of others towards a positive emancipatory *Leitkultur*, which alone can sustain an authentic coexistence and mixing of different cultures, and to engage in the forthcoming battle for that *Leitkultur. Do not simply respect others, but offer them a common struggle, since our most pressing problems today are problems we have in common.*

CHAPTER FIVE

Welcome to the Desert
of Post-Ideology

During a recent visit to California, I attended a party at a professor's house with a Slovene friend, a heavy smoker. Late in the evening, my friend became desperate and politely asked the host if he could step out onto the veranda for a smoke. When the host (no less politely) said no, my friend proposed to step out onto the street, but even this was rejected by the host who claimed that such a public display of smoking might damage his reputation with his neighbors. But what really surprised me was that, after dinner, the host offered us soft drugs, and this kind of smoking went on without any problem—as if drugs were far less dangerous than cigarettes.

The impasses of today's consumerism provide a clear case of the Lacanian distinction between pleasure and enjoyment: what Lacan calls "enjoyment" (*jouissance*) is a deadly excess rather than pleasure; its place is beyond the pleasure principle. In other words, the term *plus-de-jouir* (surplus- or excess-enjoyment) is a pleonasm, since enjoyment is in itself excessive, in contrast to pleasure, which is by definition moderate, regulated by a proper measure. We thus have two extremes: on the one hand, the enlightened hedonist who carefully calculates his pleasures to prolong his fun and avoid getting hurt; on the other hand, the *jouisseur* proper, ready to consummate his very existence in the deadly excess of enjoyment. Or, in terms of our society, on the one hand the consumerist calculating his pleasures, well protected from all kinds of harassment and threats to health; on the other, the drug addict (or smoker) bent on self-destruction. Enjoyment serves nothing, and the great effort of our contemporary hedonist-utilitarian "permissive" society is to incorporate this un(ac)countable excess into the field of (ac)counting.

Along these lines, Lee Edelman has developed the notion of homosexuality as involving an ethics of "now," of unconditional fidelity to *jouissance*, of following the death drive by totally ignoring any reference to the future or engagement with the practical complex of worldly affairs. Homosexuality thus stands for the thorough acceptance of the negativity of the death drive, of withdrawal from reality into the Real of the "Night of the World." Along these lines, Edelman opposes the radical ethics of homosexuality to the predominant obsession with posterity (that is, children): children are the "pathological" moment that binds us to pragmatic considerations and thus compels us to betray the radical ethics of *jouissance*.[1]

The first conclusion to be drawn from this is that we should reject the common-sense assumption according to which, in a hedonist-consumerist society, everyone has something to enjoy: the basic function of enlightened consumerist hedonism is, on the contrary, to deprive enjoyment of its excessive dimension, of its disturbing surplus, of the fact it serves nothing. Enjoyment is tolerated, solicited even, but on condition that it remains healthy, that it does not threaten our psychic or biological stability: chocolate yes, but fat-free; Coke yes, but diet; mayonnaise yes, but without cholesterol; sex yes, but safe sex. We are here in the domain of what Lacan calls the discourse of University, as opposed to the discourse of the Master: the Master goes to the end in his consumption, unconstrained by petty utilitarian considerations (which is why there is a certain formal homology between the traditional aristocratic master and a drug addict focused on his deadly enjoyment), while the consumerist's pleasures are regulated by scientific knowledge propagated by the University discourse. The decaffeinated enjoyment we thus obtain is a semblance of enjoyment, not its Real, and it is in this sense that Lacan talks about the imitation of enjoyment in the discourse of the University. One prototype for this discourse is the multiplicity of articles in popular magazines advocating sex as good for our health: sexual activity works like jogging, strengthening the heart, relaxing our tensions—even kissing is good

---

1   See Lee Edelman, *No Future: Queer Theory and the Death Drive*, Durham: Duke University Press 2005.

for our health. A similar celebration of desexualized vitality abounds in Stalinism. Although the total mobilization during the first five-year plan tended to oppose sexuality as the last domain of bourgeois resistance, this did not prevent it from trying to recuperate sexual energy in order to reinvigorate the struggle for socialism: in the early 1930s, a variety of tonics were widely advertised in the Soviet media, with names like "Spermin-pharmakon," "Spermol," and "Sekar fluid—Extractum testiculorum."[2] Similarly, in today's Western societies, we see the proliferation of caffeine drinks supposed to give a powerful charge of "energy" (Red Bull, etcetera).

Lacan gives us a precise insight into how the paternal prohibition functions: "In fact, the image of the ideal Father is a neurotic's fantasy. Beyond the Mother ... stands out the image of a father who would turn a blind eye to desires. This marks—more than it reveals—the true function of the Father, which is fundamentally to unite (and not to oppose) a desire to the Law."[3] While prohibiting his son's escapades, the father discreetly not only ignores and tolerates them, but even solicits them—as with the Catholic Church, which today turns a blind eye to pedophilia. We should link this insight to Lacan's critique of Hegel's notion that it is the Master who enjoys, while the servant works, being compelled to renounce enjoyment: for Lacan, on the contrary, the only enjoyments are the little bits left to the servant by the Master when he turns a blind eye to the servant's little transgressions: "*Jouissance* comes easy to the slave, and it leaves work in serfdom."[4]

An anecdote about Catherine the Great illustrates the point. On being informed that her servants were stealing wine and food behind her back, even going so far as to mock her, she just smiled, aware that occasionally dropping crumbs of enjoyment for them kept them in their position as servants. The servant's belief is that he only gets little crumbs of enjoyment, while the Master enjoys fully—in reality, however, the only enjoyment is the servant's.[5] It is in this sense that the Father as the agent of prohibition or the law sustains desire or pleasure: there is no direct access to enjoyment since its very space is

2   See Andrey Platonov, *The Foundation Pit*, New York: NYRB 2009, Translator's Notes, p. 206.

3   Jacques Lacan, *Ecrits*, New York: Norton 2007, p. 824.

4   Ibid., p. 811.

5   The ultimate story of servants' freedom and pleasure is definitely Robert Walser's *Jakob von Gunten*, New York: NYRB Classics 1999.

opened up by the blanks of the Father's controlling gaze. A negative proof for this constitutive role of the Father in carving out the space for a viable enjoyment can be found in the deadlock of today's permissiveness, where the master or expert no longer prohibits enjoyment but enjoins it ("sex is healthy," etcetera), thereby effectively sabotaging it. Indeed, as Freud once remarked to his close friend Otto Bauer, a key figure of Austrian Social Democracy (and the brother of Ida, the legendary "Dora"): "Do not try and make men happy, they do not wish happiness."[6]

What, then, is the status of the Real of *jouissance*? Is it just a presupposed virtual or fantasmatic point (like the Master's *jouissance* presupposed by the servant) or a direct Real that threatens to overwhelm us, destroying the symbolic texture? We should maintain this "undecidability," in no way reducing the Real of *jouissance* to a fantasmatic point of reference: the Real of *jouissance* effectively overwhelms the subject in psychosis. The only way to sustain the Real when it gets too close—that is, the only way to avoid psychosis—is to fictionalize it. Today, the threat of the over-proximity of the Real appears in the guise of two exceptions in the happy universe of healthy enjoyment: cigarettes and, up to a point, drugs. For different (mostly ideological) reasons, it proved impossible to "sublate" the pleasure of smoking into a healthy and useful pursuit: smoking remains a lethal addiction, a feature that obliterates all its other characteristics (it can help me relax, socialize more easily...). The strengthening of the prohibition on smoking is easily discernible in the gradual changes made to the obligatory warnings on cigarette packets: years ago, it was usually a neutral expert statement like the surgeon general's warning: "Smoking may seriously damage your health." More recently, the tone has become more and more aggressive, shifting from the University discourse to the Master's direct injunction: "Smoking kills!"—a clear warning that excess enjoyment is lethal; furthermore, the warning is printed larger and larger on the packs and accompanied by graphic photos.

The best indicator of this change in the status of smoking is, as usual, Hollywood. After the gradual dissolution of the Hays code from the late 1950s onwards, when all taboos (on homosexuality, explicit sex, drugs, and so on) were suspended, one taboo gradually imposed

---

6   Quoted from Lisa Appignanesi and John Forrester, *Freud's Women*, London: Phoenix 1992, p. 166.

itself as a new prohibition, a kind of replacement for the multiple prohibitions of the old code: smoking. Back in the classic Hollywood films of the 1930s and '40s, smoking on screen was not only totally normal, it even functioned as one of the great seduction techniques (recall, in *To Have and Have Not*, Lauren Bacall asking Humphrey Bogart for a light). Today, the only people who smoke on screen are Arab terrorists, and assorted other criminals or anti-heroes, and the possibility of digitally erasing cigarettes from classic movies has even been discussed. This new prohibition itself indicates a broader shift in the status of ethics: where the Hays code focused on ideology, enforcing sexual and social codes, the new ethics focuses on health: the bad is what threatens our health and well-being.[7]

Symptomatic here is the ambiguous role of the "electronic cigarette," which functions like sugarless sugar: an electrical device that simulates tobacco smoking by producing an inhaled mist with the physical sensation, appearance, and often the flavor and nicotine content of inhaled tobacco smoke, though without its odor, and apparently without (most of) its health risks. Most e-cigarettes are self-contained cylindrical devices the size of a ballpoint pen, designed to resemble actual cigarettes or cigars. The e-cigarette is proving difficult to classify and to regulate. Is it itself a drug? A medical product? Some airlines, for instance, have banned them because they display "addictive behavior" that may upset other passengers; others will offer them for sale during the flight.

But who is this Other whose addictive behavior—in short, whose display of excessive enjoyment—disturbs us so much? It is none other than what, in the Judeo-Christian tradition, is called the Neighbor. A neighbor by definition harasses, and "harassment" is another of those words that, although it seems to refer to a clearly defined fact, functions in a deeply ambiguous way and perpetrates an ideological mystification. What is the inner logic of the standard discourse regarding sexual harassment? The very asymmetry of seduction—the imbalance between desire and its object—is rejected. At every stage in an erotic relationship, only contractual reciprocity with mutual agreement is allowed. In this way, sexual intercourse is desexualized and becomes a "deal," in the sense of a market exchange of equivalents

---

7 I rely here on Jela Krecic, *Philosophy, Film, Fantasy* (doctoral thesis), University of Ljubljana 2008.

between equal and free partners, where the object of exchange is pleasure. The theoretical expression of this turn to pleasure is marked by the shift from Freud/Lacan to Foucault: from sexuality and desire to desexualized pleasures striving to reach the extreme of the raw Real. The explosive expansion of pornography in the digital media is exemplary of this de-sexualization of sex. The promise is "always more sex," to show it all, more and more of the raw Real, from extreme fisting (a favorite of Foucault's) to snuff movies, but all it delivers is an endlessly reproduced void and a pseudo-satisfaction. The only satisfaction one can get from this reduction of sexuality to a gynecological display of the interaction of sexual organs is an idiotic masturbatory *jouissance*.[8]

Within such a libidinal economy, the relationship to the Other is gradually replaced by what the late Lacan baptized with the neologism *les lathouses*—consumerist object-gadgets that captivate the libido with the promise of delivering excessive pleasure, but which actually reproduce only the lack itself. A couple of decades ago, a charming beer advertisement was shown on British TV. Its first part staged the well-known fairy-tale scene: a girl walks along a stream, sees a frog, takes it gently into her lap, kisses it, upon which, of course, the frog turns miraculously into a handsome young man. The story did not end there however: the young man then embraces and kisses the girl, who promptly turns into a bottle of beer, which the man holds triumphantly in his hand. For the woman, the point is that her love and affection (signaled by the kiss) turns an ugly frog into a beautiful man, a full phallic presence; for the man, the point is to reduce the woman to a partial object, the cause of his desire (the *objet petit a*). The unexpected reversal here thus perfectly exemplifies the shift from neighbor to *lathouse*.

Likewise, the rise of political correctness and the increase in interpersonal violence represent two sides of the same coin. Jean-Claude Milner has argued that insofar as the basic premise of

---

8   I rely here on Serge Andre, *No Sex, No Future*, Paris: La Muette 2010 pp. 45–51. A French documentary released at the beginning of 2012, with the Lacanian title *Il n'y a pas de rapport sexuel* (dir. Raphael Siboni), is much more than a "making of" a hardcore porn movie: by following from a minimal distance the shooting of a hardcore film, it totally desexualizes the entire scene, presenting hardcore acting as grey repetitive work: faking ecstatic pleasure, masturbating off scene to retain an erection, smoking during the breaks—an anxiety producing procedure.

political correctness is the reduction of sexuality to a contractual mutual consent, the gay rights movement unavoidably reaches its climax in contracts that stipulate extreme forms of sadomasochistic sex (treating a person like a dog on a lead, slave-trading, torture, even consensual killing).[9] In such practices, the market freedom of the contract sublates itself: slave-trading becomes the ultimate assertion of freedom. It is as if the motif of "Kant with Sade" becomes reality in an unexpected way.

Two things are thus clear. First, if Thomas de Quincey had to rewrite the opening lines of his famous essay *Murder Considered as One of the Fine Arts* today, he would undoubtedly change the final word (procrastination): "If once a man indulges himself in murder, very soon he comes to think little of robbing; and from robbing he comes next to drinking and Sabbath-breaking, and from that to incivility *and smoking in public*." Second, the underlying problem here is that of loving one's neighbor—as usual, G. K. Chesterton hit the nail on the head: "The Bible tells us to love our neighbours, and also to love our enemies; probably because they are generally the same people." So what happens when these problematic neighbors strike back?

Although the UK riots of August 2011 were triggered by the suspicious death of Mark Duggan, it is generally accepted that they expressed a deeper unease—but of what kind? Similar to the riots in the Paris suburbs in 2005, the UK protesters had no message to deliver. The contrast with the massive student demonstrations of November 2010, which also turned violent, is clear. The students had a message—the rejection of the government's higher education reforms. This is why it is difficult to conceive of the 2011 riots in Marxist terms, as indicative of an emerging revolutionary subject; much more appropriate here is the Hegelian notion of the "rabble"—referring to those outside the organized social sphere, prevented from participating in social production, who are able to express their discontent only in the form of "irrational" outbursts of destructive violence, or what Hegel called "abstract negativity." Perhaps this is the hidden truth of Hegel, of his political thought: the more a society conforms to a well-organized rational state, the more the abstract negativity of "irrational" violence returns.

---

9   Jean-Claude Milner, *Clartés de tout*, Paris: Verdier 2011, p. 98.

We were told that the events of 1989–91—the disintegration of the Communist regimes—signaled the end of ideology. The era of grand ideological projects that inevitably ended in totalitarian catastrophe was over, as we entered a new era of pragmatic rational politics, and so forth. However, if the commonplace that we live in a post-ideological era has any sense at all, it is here, in these ongoing outbursts of violence, that it becomes discernible. During the UK riots of 2011, no particular demands were made by the protestors: what we had was a zero-level protest, a violent act which demands nothing. There was an irony in watching the sociologists, intellectuals, and commentators trying to understand and to help. Trying desperately to translate the protests back into their familiar language, they only succeeded in obfuscating the key enigma the riots presented.

The protesters, although effectively underprivileged and de facto excluded, were in no sense living on the edge of starvation or reduced to the level of bare survival. People in much more terrible material straits, even in conditions of physical and ideological oppression, have been able to organize themselves into political agents with clear agendas. The fact that the protests had no program is thus itself a fact to be interpreted, one that tells us a great deal about our ideologico-political predicament: what kind of universe do we inhabit that can celebrate itself as a society of choice, but in which the only alternative available to an enforced democratic consensus is a form of blind acting out? The sad fact that opposition to the system cannot articulate itself in the guise of a realistic alternative, or at least a coherent utopian project, but only takes the form of meaningless outburst, is a grave indictment of our epoch. What function does our celebrated freedom of choice serve when the only choice is effectively between playing by the rules and (self-)destructive violence?

Alain Badiou has claimed that we live in a social space that is progressively experienced as "worldless": within such a space, meaningless violence is the only form protest can take. Even Nazi anti-Semitism opened up a world, however ghastly: it described its situation by positing an enemy, the "Jewish conspiracy"; it named a goal and the means of achieving it. Nazism disclosed reality in a way that allowed its subjects to acquire a global cognitive map, which included a space for their meaningful engagement. Perhaps it is here that we should locate one of the main dangers of capitalism. Although capitalism is global, encompassing the whole world, it sustains a *stricto sensu* "worldless" ideological constellation, depriving the vast majority of people of any meaningful cognitive orientation. Capitalism is the first socio-economic order which *de-totalizes meaning*: it is not global at the level of meaning. There is, after all, no global "capitalist worldview," no "capitalist civilization" proper. The fundamental lesson of globalization is precisely that capitalism can accommodate itself to all civilizations, from Christian to Hindu or Buddhist, from West to East. Capitalism's global dimension can only be formulated at the level of truth-without-meaning, as the real of the global market mechanism.

This is why both conservative and liberal reactions to the UK riots clearly missed the mark. The conservative reaction was predictable: there is no justification for such vandalism, all necessary means to restore order must be used, and what is needed to prevent further explosions of this kind is not more tolerance and social intervention but more discipline, hard work and a sense of responsibility. What is false in this account is not only that it neglects the desperate social situation that drives young people to such violent outbursts, but, perhaps more important, the way those outbursts echo the subterranean premises of conservative ideology itself. When, back in the 1990s, the British Conservative Party launched its infamous Back to Basics campaign, its obscene supplement was clearly indicated by Norman Tebbitt, "never shy about exposing the dirty secrets of the Conservative unconscious": "man is not just a social but also a territorial animal; it must be part of our agenda to satisfy those basic instincts of tribalism and territoriality."[10] This, then, is what Back to Basics was really about: the reassertion of the barbaric "basic instincts" lurking beneath the semblance of civilized bourgeois society. And do we not encounter in the recent violent outbursts these same basic instincts—not of the lower underprivileged strata, but of the hegemonic capitalist ideology itself?

Even further back, in the 1960s, Herbert Marcuse introduced the concept of "repressive desublimation" to explain the "sexual revolution": human drives can be desublimated, deprived of their civilized coating, and still retain their "repressive" character—is not this kind of "repressive desublimation" what we see on British streets today? Not

---

10   See Jacqueline Rose, *States of Fantasy*, Oxford: Oxford University Press 1996, p. 149.

men reduced to "natural beasts," but the historically specific "natural beast" produced by capitalist ideology itself, the zero-level of the capitalist subject. In Seminar XVIII (*Le savoir du psychanalyste*, 1970–71, unpublished), Lacan plays with the idea of a specific capitalist discourse (or discourse of the capitalist) that is the same as the discourse of the Master, but with the first (left) couple exchanging places: $ occupies the place of the agent and the Master-Signifier the place of truth:

$$\frac{\$}{S_1} \frac{S_2}{a}$$

The connecting lines remain the same as in the Master's discourse ($\$—a, S_1—S_2$), but they run diagonally: while the agent is the same as in the discourse of the Hysteric, the (divided) subject, it does not address itself to the Master, but to the surplus-enjoyment, the "product" of capitalist circulation. As in the discourse of the Master, the "other" is here the Servant's Knowledge (or, increasingly, scientific knowledge), dominated by the true Master, capital itself.[11]

The UK's urban violence thus cannot be accounted for merely by poverty and a lack of horizons, or the dissolution of the family and other social links. As to the form of subjectivity that fits this constellation, we might begin with "The Stranger," the famous prose poem by Baudelaire:

> Tell me, enigmatical man, whom do you love best, your father,
> Your mother, your sister, or your brother?
> I have neither father, nor mother, nor sister, nor brother.
> Your friends?
> Now you use a word whose meaning I have never known.
> Your country?
> I do not know in what latitude it lies.
> Beauty?
> I could indeed love her, Goddess and Immortal.
> Gold?
> I hate it as you hate God.
> Then, what do you love, extraordinary stranger?

---

11   See Nestor Braunstein, "Le discours capitaliste, 'cinquième discours'?," *Savoirs et Clinique* 14 (2011), pp. 94–100.

I love the clouds … the clouds … that pass … up there … up there
… the wonderful clouds![12]

Does this "enigmatical man" not provide the portrait of an internet
geek? Alone in front of the screen, he has neither father nor mother,
neither country nor god—all he needs is a digital cloud to which his
internet device is linked. The final outcome of such a position is, of
course, that the subject itself turns into "a cloud in pants," avoiding
sexual contact as too intrusive. In 1915, Vladimir Mayakovsky entered
a train carriage in which the only other occupant was a young woman;
to put her at ease he introduced himself by saying, "I am not a man but
a cloud in pants." As the words left his lips he realized the phrase was
perfect for a poem and went on to write his first masterpiece, "A Cloud
in Pants":[13]

> No longer a man with a mission,
> something wet
> and tender
> — a cloud in pants.

How, then, does such a "cloud in pants" have sex? An ad in the United
Airlines in-flight magazine begins with a suggestion: "Maybe it's time
to outsource … your dating life." It goes on: "People hire professionals
to handle so many aspects of their lives, so why not use a professional
to help you find someone special? We are matchmaking professionals—this is what we do day in and day out."[14] After outsourcing
manual work (and much of the pollution) to Third World countries,
after outsourcing (most) torture to dictatorships (whose torturers
were probably trained by US or Chinese specialists), after outsourcing
our political life to administrative experts (who are obviously less and
less up to the task—see the morons who compete in Republican Party
primaries)—why not take this process to its logical conclusion and
consider outsourcing sex itself? Why burden ourselves with the effort
of seduction with all its potential embarrassments? After a woman and

---

12   Charles Baudelaire, *Paris Spleen*, trans. Louise Varese, New York: New
Directions 1970, p.1.
13   Quoted from http://cloud-in-trousers.blogspot.com.
14   United Airlines, *Hemispheres* magazine, July 2011, p. 135.

I agree to have sex, each of us need only designate a younger stand-in, so that while they make love (or, more precisely, while the two of us make love through them), we can have a quiet drink and conversation and then retire to our own quarters to rest or to read a good book. After such disengagement, the only way to reconnect with reality is, of course, through raw violence.

The left-liberal response to the riots, no less predictably, was to stick to their mantra about neglected social programs and integration efforts, the failure of which has deprived the younger generation of immigrants of any decent economic and social prospects. Instead of indulging in conservative revenge fantasies, we should make the effort to understand the deeper causes of their violent outbursts: can we even imagine what it means to be a young man living in a poor and racially mixed area, a priori suspected and harassed by the police, surrounded by destitution and broken families, not only unemployed but often unemployable, with no hope for the future? The moment we take all this into account, the reasons why people are taking to the streets become clear—supposedly. The problem with this account is that it merely lists the objective conditions for the riots, ignoring the subjective dimension: to riot is to make a subjective statement, implicitly to declare how one relates to one's objective conditions, how one subjectivizes them. We live in an era of cynicism in which we can easily imagine a protester who, having been caught looting and burning and pressed for the reasons for his violence, will suddenly start to talk like a social worker, sociologist or social psychologist, citing diminished social mobility, rising economic insecurity, the disintegration of paternal authority, the lack of maternal love in his early childhood. He knows what he is doing, but he does it nonetheless, as in the famous "Gee, Officer Krupke" song from Leonard Bernstein's *West Side Story* (lyrics by Stephen Sondheim), which contains the line "Juvenile delinquency is purely a social disease":

> We never had the love
> That every child oughta get
> We ain't no delinquents
> We're misunderstood
> Deep down inside us there is good

…
My daddy beats my mommy
My mommy clobbers me
My grandpa is a commie
My grandma pushes tea
My sister wears a mustache
My brother wears a dress
Goodness gracious, that's why I'm a mess

…
This boy don't need a couch
He needs a useful career
Society's played him a terrible trick
And sociologically he's sick

…
They tell me get a job
Like be a soda jerker
Which means I'd be a slob
It's not I'm antisocial
I'm only anti-work

Such subjects do not simply represent a social disease, they declare themselves to be incarnations of one, ironically staging different accounts of their predicament (just how a social worker, a psychologist, a judge would describe it). Consequently, it is meaningless to ponder which of the two reactions to the riots, conservative or liberal, is worse: as Stalin would have put it, they are *both* worse, and this includes the warning voiced by both sides about the real danger of these outbursts residing in the easily predictable racist *reaction* of the "silent majority." This reaction (which should absolutely not be dismissed as simply reactionary) already took place in the guise of a "tribal" activity of its own, as local communities (Turkish, Afro-Caribbean, Sikh …) quickly formed their own vigilante units to protect their hard-earned property. Here, too, we should reject the injunctions regarding which side to take in this conflict: are the small shop-keepers defending the petty bourgeoisie against a genuine if violent protest against the system, or are they representatives of the genuine working class resisting the forces of social disintegration? The protesters' violence was almost exclusively directed against their own. The cars burned and the stores looted were not those of richer neighborhoods, they were the hard-won acquisitions of the very stratum from which the protesters originated. The sad truth of the situation lies in this conflict between two poles of the underprivileged: those who still succeed in functioning within the system and those who are too frustrated to go on doing so and are only able to strike out at the other pole of their own community. The conflict that sustains the riots is thus not simply a conflict between different parts of society; it is, at its most radical, *a conflict between non-society and society*, between those who have nothing to lose and those who have everything to lose, between those without a stake in their community and those whose stakes are the greatest.

But why were the protesters pushed towards this kind of violence? Zygmunt Bauman was on the right track here when he characterized the riots as acts of "defective and disqualified consumers." More than anything else, the riots were a consumerist carnival of destruction, an expression of acquisitive desire violently enacted when unable to realize itself in the "proper" way (by shopping). As such, of course, the riots also contain a moment of genuine protest, a kind of ironic reply to the consumerist ideology by which we are bombarded in our daily lives: "You call on us to consume while simultaneously depriving us of the possibility of doing so properly—so here we are doing it the only way open to us!" The violence thus, in a sense, staged the truth of our "post-ideological society," displaying in a painfully palpable way the material force of ideology. The problem with the riots was not their violence as such, but the fact that it was not truly self-assertive— in Nietzschean terms, it was reactive, not active, impotent rage and despair masked as a display of force, envy masked as a triumphant carnival.

One danger is that religion will come to fill this void and restore meaning. That is to say, the riots need to be situated in the series they form with another type of violence perceived by the liberal majority as a threat to our way of life: terrorist attacks and suicide bombings. In both instances, violence and counter-violence are caught up in a deadly vicious circle, each generating the very forces it tries to combat. In both cases, we are dealing with blind *passages à l'acte*, where the recourse to violence is an implicit admission of impotence. The difference is that, in contrast to the Paris or UK riots conceived as "zero-level" protests, violent outbursts that demanded nothing, terrorist attacks are carried out on behalf of the *absolute* Meaning provided by religion.

But then there are the Arab uprisings. Do they not offer an example of a collective act of resistance that avoids this false alternative between self-destructive violence and religious fundamentalism?

CHAPTER SIX

The Arab Winter, Spring, Summer, and Fall

The item numbered PO 24.1999 in the Museum of Islamic Art in Doha is a simple tenth-century circular earthenware dish from Iran or Central Asia (Nishapur or Samarqand), its diameter 43 cm, decorated in black writing on a white slip ground with a proverb attributed to Yahya ibn Ziyad: "Foolish is the person who misses his chance and afterwards reproaches fate." Such dishes were meant to solicit an appropriate conversation among learned men during and after the meal—a forgotten art whose last great practitioner was perhaps Immanuel Kant, and a practice foreign to our fast-food times, which know only business meals ("power lunches"), not thinking meals.

Furthermore, such an integration of the dish (as art object) into its environs (the meal) is a general feature of Muslim art, in clear contrast to the standard European practice of isolating the art object in the sacred space of the exhibition hall, abstracting it from daily activities (hence, for Duchamp, the urinal became an object of art the moment it was displayed in an art gallery). Pei, the architect of the Museum of Islamic Art building, understood this feature. When he struggled with the basic principles of his design, he realized that, instead of treating the play of sun and shadow as a disturbing element, he should integrate it into his project. If we imagine the MIA building simply as a building and abstract from how the play of brightness and darkness affects our perception of it, we get an incomplete object—the line that separates the parts in dazzling sunshine and the parts that remain in shadow is an integral part of the building. And the same goes for our dish: in order to fully grasp it as a work of art, we must locate it in the process of eating.

The people who ate from the dish followed a specific temporal rhythm: its message is gradually revealed as the food disappears. There is, however, a more complex process at work here, since when the dish is full, one can probably already read the proverb written on the edges; what is then gradually revealed is the drawing in the center, clearly a symbol of the circularity of life similar to the famous image of a snake eating its own tail. But is this "great circle of life" the ultimate message of the dish? What if the central drawing is rather a kind of empty symbol pretending to deliver a profound ultimate truth, but effectively providing only a platitude characteristic of a pseudo-wisdom?

In other words, is not the circular drawing at the center like those deep tautologies ("life is life," "everything that is born has to die," etcetera) that merely mask our basic perplexity as a supposedly profound wisdom? We use such phrases when we do not know what to say, but want nonetheless to sound wise. The platitudinous nature of such wisdom reveals itself in the opportunism of proverbs: whatever happens, you can accompany it with an appropriate proverb. If someone takes a big risk and succeeds, you can say, "Only those who take great risks achieve something great!"; if he fails, you can say, "You cannot piss against the wind!" or "The higher they fly, the harder they fall!" and, again, it will seem profound. Another proof of the vacuity of such proverbial wisdom is that no matter how you turn it around the result will always sound wise. "Don't get caught up in the vanity of earthly life and its pleasures, think about eternity as the only true life!" sounds deep, but then so does "Don't try to grasp the rainbow of eternity, enjoy your terrestrial life, it is the only life you have!" But what about "A wise man does not oppose eternity to terrestrial life, he is able to see the ray of eternity shining through in our ordinary lives!"? Or, again, "A wise man accepts the gap that separates our terrestrial life from eternity, he knows that we mortals cannot bring the two together—only god can do it!"?

The proverb on the edge of the dish, however, is precisely *not* such a form of wisdom. "Foolish is the person who misses his chance and afterwards reproaches fate." Let us turn it around: "Foolish is the person who, having missed his chance, does not see that his failure was the work of fate." This statement is simply a religious commonplace, which tells us that really nothing is up to chance, that everything is decided by an inscrutable fate. But the proverb on the dish, read closely, does not say the opposite of this commonplace: its message is not simply: "There is no fate, everything is chance." What then is its message? Consider again the temporal dimension of using the dish: when, at the beginning of the meal, the dinner guests first notice the inscription on the edges of the full dish, they dismiss it as a lesson on the opportunism involved in seizing a chance; however, once the dish is empty, they see that the true hidden message is a platitude, and realize they have missed the truth in the first inscription. So they return to it, read it again, and only then does it strike them that it is not about chance versus fate, but about something much more complex and interesting: about how it is in their power to *choose their fate*.

In the suburbs of Doha there is a camp for immigrant workers. The lowest among them on the social scale come from Nepal. They are only free to visit the city center on Fridays; on Fridays, however, single men are prohibited from visiting shopping malls—officially to maintain the family spirit in the malls, but this is of course only an excuse, the real reason being to prevent the immigrants from mingling with the wealthier shoppers. (Immigrant workers live alone in Qatar; they are neither allowed nor can afford to bring their families with them.)

Let us then step down from the archaeological and art-historical heights into ordinary life and imagine a group of poor Nepali workers resting on the grass south of the central souk in Doha on a Friday. They are eating a modest meal of humus and bread from our dish, gradually emptying it until the message of Yahya ibn Ziyad becomes clear. Engaging in conversation, one of them says: "But what if this applies also to us? What if it is not our fate to live here as outcasts? What if, instead of bemoaning our fate, we should seize the moment and change it?"

This radical emancipatory potential of Islam is not a fiction—it can be detected in an unexpected place: the Haitian Revolution, a truly "defining moment in world history." Haiti was an exception from the very beginning of its revolutionary fight against slavery, which ended in independence in January 1804: "Only in Haiti was the declaration of human freedom universally consistent. Only in Haiti was this declaration sustained at all costs, in direct opposition to the social order and economic logic of the day." For this reason, "there is no single event in the whole of modern history whose implications were more threatening to the dominant global order of things."[1] It is little known that one of the organizers of the Haiti rebellion was a black slave preacher known as John Bookman, a name designating him as literate, and—surprise, surprise—the "book" the name refers to was not the Bible but the Qur'an.

This brings to mind the great tradition of millenarian "Communist" rebellions in Islam, especially the "Qarmatian republic" and the Zanj revolt. The Qarmatians were a millenarian Ismaili group centered in eastern Arabia (today's Bahrain), where they established a utopian republic in 899. They are often denounced for having instigated a "century of terrorism": during the 930 Hajj season, they seized the Black Stone from Mecca—an act taken to signal that the age of love had arrived, so one no longer had to obey the Law. The Qarmatians' goal was to build a society based on reason and equality. The state was governed by a council of six, with a chief who was first among equals. All property within the community was distributed evenly among all initiates. Although the Qarmatians were organized as an esoteric society, they were not a secret one: their activities were public and openly propagated. Their rise was instigated by the slave rebellion in Basra, which disrupted the power of Baghdad. This "Zanj Revolt," which took place over a period of fifteen years (869–83), involved over 500,000 slaves who had been imported to the region from across the Muslim empire. Their leader, a black slave called Ali ibn Muhammad, was shocked by the suffering of the slaves working in the Basra marshes, and began to inquire into their working conditions and nutritional standards. He claimed to be a descendent of the Caliph Ali ibn Abu Talib; when his claim was not accepted, he began to preach a radically egalitarian doctrine according to which the most qualified man should reign, even if he was an Abyssinian slave—no wonder that, as ever, the official historians (such as Al-Tabari and Al-Masudi) noted only the "vicious and brutal" character of the uprising.

Returning to the scene of the Nepali workers, why should we not take a step further and imagine a woman (also an immigrant worker, say, who works as a hotel cleaner) who serves them food on our dish? The fact that it is a woman who brings them not only food to eat but also food for thought (the message on the dish) is of a special

---

1   Peter Hallward, *Damming the Flood*, London: Verso 2007, p. 13.

significance with regard to the role of women in Islam. Muhammad first experienced his revelations as poetic hallucinations, to which his immediate reaction was: "Now none of God's creatures was more hateful to me than an ecstatic poet or a man possessed." The first believer in his message—the first Muslim, and the one who saved him from both unbearable uncertainty and the role of village idiot—was Khadija, *a woman*. So what if the woman serving the immigrant workers has wisely chosen this particular dish to remind the men of the truth that her own subordination to their masters is also not a question of fate—or, rather, that it is a fate that can be changed? We can see how, although Islam has recently had bad press in the West for the way it treats women, a quite different potential lies concealed beneath the patriarchal surface.

This, then, is the ultimate message of the item numbered PO 24.1999 in the Museum of Islamic Art: insofar as we tend to oppose East and West in terms of fate and freedom, Islam stands for a third position that undermines this binary opposition—neither subordination to blind Fate nor freedom to do what one wants, both of which presuppose an abstract external opposition between the two terms, but rather a deeper freedom to decide ("choose") our fate. The events of 2011 in the Middle East amply demonstrate that this legacy is alive and well: to find a "good" Islam, we do not have to go back to the tenth century; we have it right here, unfolding in front of our eyes.

When an authoritarian regime approaches its final crisis, as a rule its dissolution follows two steps. Before its actual collapse, a mysterious rupture takes place: all of a sudden, people know that the game is over, and they are simply no longer afraid. It is not only that the regime loses its legitimacy; its exercise of power is itself perceived as an impotent panic reaction. In *Shah of Shahs*, a classic account of the Khomeini revolution, Ryszard Kapuściński located the precise moment of this rupture: at a Tehran crossroad, a single demonstrator refused to budge when a policeman shouted at him, and the embarrassed policeman simply withdrew. Within a couple of hours, the whole of Tehran had heard about the incident, and although the subsequent street-fighting went on for weeks, everyone somehow knew the game was over.

Was something similar going on after Moussavi lost to Ahmadinejad in the rigged Iranian elections of 2009? There are many versions of what took place. Some saw the protests as the culmination of the pro-Western "reform movement" along the lines of the "orange" revolutions in Ukraine, Georgia, etcetera—a secular reaction to the Khomeini revolution. They supported the protests as the first step towards a new liberal-democratic Iran free of Muslim fundamentalism. They were counteracted by skeptics who believed that Ahmadinejad had genuinely won: he was the voice of the majority, while Moussavi's support came from the middle classes and their gilded youth. In short, they argued, let's drop the illusions and face the fact that, in Ahmadinejad, Iran has the president it deserves. Then there were those who dismissed Moussavi as a member of the clerical establishment whose differences with Ahmadinejad were merely cosmetic: Moussavi also wanted to continue the atomic energy program, he was against recognizing Israel, and he had enjoyed the full support of Khomeini as prime minister during the war with Iraq, when all democracy was suppressed.

Finally, saddest of all were the leftist supporters of Ahmadinejad. For them, what was really at stake was Iranian independence. Ahmadinejad had won because he had stood up for the country's independence, exposed elite corruption, and used oil wealth to boost the incomes of the poor majority. This was, so we were told, the true Ahmadinejad beneath the Western media's image of a Holocaust-denying fanatic. According to this view, what was effectively going on in Iran was a repetition of the 1953 overthrow of Mossadegh—a Western-financed coup against a legitimate president. But this view not only ignored facts—the high level of electoral participation (up from the usual 55 percent to 85 percent) can only be explained as a protest vote—it also displayed its blindness to a genuine demonstration of popular will, patronizingly assuming that, for the backward Iranians, Ahmadinejad was as good as they were going to get, not being mature enough to be governed by a secular leftist leader.

Opposed as they are, all these versions of the Iranian protests read them in terms of Islamic hardliners versus pro-Western liberal reformists, which is why they find it so difficult to locate Moussavi: is he a Western-backed reformer who wants more personal freedom and a market economy, or a member of the clerical establishment whose eventual victory would not affect the nature of the regime in any significant way? Such extreme oscillations show that they all miss the true nature of the protests.

The green color adopted by Moussavi supporters, and the cries of "Allahu akbar!" resounding from the roofs of Tehran in the evening darkness, clearly indicated that they saw their protest as a repetition of the 1979 Khomeini revolution, as a return to its roots, an undoing of the revolution's later corruption. This return to roots was not only programmatic; it also concerned, even more so, the behavior of the crowds: the emphatic demonstration of the people's unity, their all-encompassing solidarity, creative self-organization and improvisation, their unique combination of spontaneity and discipline, like the ominous march of thousands in complete silence. We were dealing with a genuine popular uprising of the disappointed partisans of the Khomeini revolution.

This is why we must compare the events in Iran to the US intervention in Iraq. The former involved a genuine assertion of the popular will, in contrast to the foreign imposition of democracy in Iraq.[2] In other words, the episode in Iran shows how things should have been done in Iraq. And this is also why the Iranian protests may be read as a comment on the platitudinous nature of Obama's 2009 speech in Cairo, which focused on the need for a dialogue between religions: no, we do not need a dialogue between religions (or civilizations); we need solidarity between those who struggle for justice in Muslim countries and those who participate in the same struggle elsewhere.

---

2   If the basic underlying axiom of the Cold War was that of MAD (Mutually Assured Destruction), the axiom of today's war on terror seems to be the opposite: that of NUTS (Nuclear Use Target Selection), that is, the idea that it is possible to destroy the enemy's nuclear capacities in a surgical strike, while our anti-missile shield protects us from any counter-attack. More precisely, the US adopts a differential strategy: it acts as if it continues to hold to the MAD logic in its relations with Russia and China, while being tempted to practice NUTS with Iran and North Korea. The paradoxical mechanism of MAD inverts the logic of the "self-realizing prophecy" into a "self-stulti-fying intention": the very fact that each side can be sure the other side will respond with full destructive force guarantees that no side will start a war. The logic of NUTS is, on the contrary, that the enemy can be forced to disarm if it is assured that we can strike at him with impunity. The very fact that two directly contradictory strategies are mobilized simultaneously by the same superpower bears witness to the fantasmatic character of this entire mode of reasoning.

In other words, we need a politicization that strengthens the struggle here, there, and everywhere.

At least two crucial consequences follow from this insight. First, Ahmadinejad is not the hero of the Islamist poor, but a genuinely corrupt Islamo-fascist populist, a kind of Iranian Berlusconi whose mixture of clownish posturing and ruthless power politics is causing unease even among the majority of the mullahs. His demagogic distribution of crumbs to the poor should not deceive us. Behind him are not only the organs of police repression and a very Westernized PR apparatus, but also a strong class of nouveau riche, the result of the regime's corruption (Iran's Revolutionary Guard is not a working-class militia, but a mega-corporation, the most powerful center of wealth in the country).

Second, one should make a clear distinction between the two main candidates opposed to Ahmadinejad, Mehdi Karroubi and Moussavi. Karroubi really is a reformist, basically proposing an Iranian version of identity politics, promising favors to all the particular groups. Moussavi is something entirely different. His name stands for a genuine resuscitation of the popular dream that sustained the Khomeini revolution. Even if this dream was utopian, we should recognize in it the genuine utopia of the revolution itself. What this means is that the 1979 revolution cannot be reduced to a hard-line Islamist takeover—it was much more. Now is the time to remember the incredible effervescence of the first year following the revolution, with its breathtaking explosion of political and social creativity, organizational experiments, and debates among students and ordinary people. The very fact that this explosion had to be stifled demonstrates that the Khomeini revolution was an authentic political event, a momentary *opening* that unleashed unprecedented forces of social transformation, a moment in which everything seemed possible. What followed was a gradual closing down with the takeover of political control by the Islamist establishment. To put it in Freudian terms, today's protest movement is the "return of the repressed" of the Khomeini revolution.

It is, however, no longer the same regime, but just one corrupted authoritarian rule among others. Ayatollah Khamenei lost whatever remained of his status as a principled spiritual leader elevated above the fray and appeared as what he actually is—just one among a horde of opportunistic politicians. However, in spite of this (temporary) outcome, it is vitally important to keep in mind that we have witnessed a great emancipatory event, one which did not conform to the framework of a struggle between pro-Western liberals and anti-Western fundamentalists. If our cynical pragmatism means that we lose the capacity to recognize this emancipatory dimension, then we in the West are effectively entering a post-democratic era, creating the conditions for our own Ahmadinejads.

What began in Iran exploded in the so-called Arab Spring, which reached its high point in Egypt. One of the cruelest ironies of the Egyptian situation was the West's concern that the transition should proceed in a "lawful" way—as if, before 2011, Egypt had enjoyed the rule of law! We should not forget that, for many long years, Egypt was in a permanent state of emergency imposed by the Mubarak regime. The rule of law was suspended, keeping the entire country in a state of political immobility, stifling genuine political life, so that it makes perfect sense that so many people on the streets of Cairo could now claim to feel alive for the first time in their lives. But the usual accusation that Western powers are now paying the price for their hypocritical support of a non-democratic regime does not reach far enough. When the Arab Spring arrived, there was no noticeable fundamentalist presence in either Tunis or Egypt—the people were simply revolting against an oppressive regime. The big question, of course, was what would happen the day after? Who would emerge as the political winner? When a new provisional government was nominated in Tunis, it excluded Islamists and the more radical left. The smug reaction of liberals was "good, since they are basically the same, two totalitarian extremes." But are things so simple? Is not the true long-term antagonism, in fact, precisely that between Islamists and the left? Even if they were for a moment united against the regime, once they approach victory, their unity will end, they will engage in deadly struggle, possibly more cruel than the fight against their shared enemy.

The civil war in Libya which followed the uprisings in Egypt and Bahrain was a clear case of renormalization: we were back in the safe waters of an anti-terrorist struggle. All attention was focused on the fate of Gaddafi, the pro-terrorist arch-villain bombing his own people, and the human rights militarists again had their day in the sun. Forgotten was the fact that, in Tahrir Square, a quarter of a million people gathered again to protest against the religious kidnapping of the uprising; forgotten was the Saudi military intervention in Bahrain, which quashed the protests of the majority against the autocratic regime—where was the West to protest against this violation of human rights? The same obscurity marks the uprising in Syria: although the Assad regime deserves no sympathy, the politico-ideological credentials of its opponents are far from clear.

From the Western standpoint, the interesting aspect of the events in Libya and Syria were the indecision and ambiguity of the occidental powers' reaction. The West directly intervened in Libya to support rebels who did not propose any emancipatory political platform (as they had in Tunisia and in Egypt); moreover, the West intervened against a regime that, over the previous decade, had fully collaborated with it, even accepting outsourced terrorist suspects for torture. In Syria, it is clear that strong geopolitical interests prevent the possibility of any strong international pressure being applied to the regime. (Israel obviously prefers Assad to any alternative.) All this points towards the key difference between Libya/Syria and the Arab Spring proper: in the former, a power struggle and rebellion were (and are) going on for which we are allowed to express our sympathies (to be against Gaddafi or Assad), but the dimension of radical emancipatory struggle is clearly missing.

Even in the case of clearly fundamentalist movements, however, we should be careful not to miss the social components. The Taliban are regularly presented as a fundamentalist Islamist group enforcing its rule with terror; however, when, in the Spring of 2009, they took over the Swat valley in Pakistan, the *New York Times* reported that they had engineered "a class revolt that exploits profound fissures between a small group of wealthy landlords and their landless tenants." The ideological bias of the *Times* article was discernible in its talk of the Taliban's "ability to exploit class divisions," as if their "true" agenda lay elsewhere—in religious fundamentalism—and they were merely "taking advantage" of the plight of the poor landless farmers. To this, one should simply add two things. First, the distinction between the "true" agenda and instrumental manipulation is externally imposed on the Taliban: as if the landless farmers themselves do not experience their plight in "fundamentalist religious" terms! Second, if by "taking advantage" of the farmers' plight the Taliban are "raising alarm about the risks to Pakistan, which remains largely feudal," what prevents liberal democrats in Pakistan as well as the US from similarly "taking advantage" of this plight and trying to help the farmers? The sad implication of the fact this obvious question was not raised in the *Times* report is that the feudal forces in Pakistan are the "natural allies" of liberal democracy.

Returning to Egypt, the most shameful and dangerously opportunistic reaction was that of Tony Blair as reported on CNN: change is necessary, he said, but it should be stable change. "Stable change" in Egypt could only mean a compromise with the Mubarak forces, who might sacrifice Mubarak himself and slightly enlarge the ruling circle. The hypocrisy of Western liberals is breathtaking: they publicly support the spread of democracy throughout the world, but now, as the people revolt against tyrants in the name of freedom and justice, and not on behalf of religion, they are "deeply concerned." Why "concern," why not joy that freedom has been given a chance? Today, more than ever, Mao Zedong's old motto is highly pertinent: "There is chaos under the heaven—the situation is excellent."

Reversing the well-known characterization of Marxism as "the Islam of the twentieth century," a secularization of Islam's abstract fanaticism, Pierre-André Taguieff has claimed that Islam is turning out to be "the Marxism of the twenty-first century," taking up, after the decline of Communism, its violent anti-capitalism. But do not the recent vicissitudes of Muslim fundamentalism confirm Walter Benjamin's old insight that "every rise of Fascism bears witness to a failed revolution"? The rise of fascism is the result of the left's failure, but simultaneously proof that there was a revolutionary potential, a dissatisfaction, which the left was not able to mobilize. And the same holds for today's so-called "Islamo-fascism," the rise of which has been exactly correlative to the disappearance of the secular left in Muslim countries. When Afghanistan is portrayed as the worst example of an Islamic fundamentalist country, who still remembers that, forty years ago, it was a country with a strong secular tradition, including a powerful Communist Party, which took power there independently of the Soviet Union? Where did this secular tradition go?

This brings us to the true, and ominous, lesson of the Tunisian and Egyptian revolts: if the moderate liberal forces continue to ignore the radical left, they will generate an insurmountable fundamentalist tidal wave. For the key liberal legacy to survive, liberals need the fraternal help of the radical left. Although (almost) everyone enthusiastically supported these democratic rebellions, there is a hidden struggle for their appropriation going on. The official circles and most of the Western media celebrate them as being essentially the same as the "pro-democracy" revolutions in Eastern Europe: a desire for Western liberal democracy, a desire to become like the West. This is why unease sets in when it becomes clear there is another dimension at work, one usually referred to as the demand for social justice. This struggle for reappropriation is not only a question of interpretation, but has crucial practical consequences. We should not be overly fascinated by sublime moments of national unity, since the key question is always: what happens afterwards? How will this emancipatory moment be translated into a new social order? As noted, over the few last decades, we have witnessed a whole series of emancipatory popular explosions which have been reappropriated by the global capitalist order, either in its liberal form (from South Africa to the Philippines) or in its fundamentalist form (Iran). We should not forget that none of the countries involved in the Arab Spring was formally democratic: they were all more or less authoritarian, so that the demand for social and economic justice was spontaneously integrated into the demand for democracy—as if poverty was the result of the greed and corruption of those in power, so that it would be enough to get rid of them. But if we get democracy and poverty still remains—what *then*?

Unfortunately, it looks increasingly likely that the Egyptian summer of 2011 will be remembered as the end of the revolution, as the suffocating of its emancipatory potential. Its grave-diggers are the army and the Islamists. That is to say, the contours of the pact between the army (which is still the good old Mubarak army, the great recipient of US financial aid) and the Islamists (who were totally marginalized in the early months of the upheaval, but regained ground subsequently) are becoming increasingly clear: the Islamists will tolerate the material privileges of the army and will be assured of ideological hegemony in return. The losers will be the pro-Western liberals (still too weak despite all the CIA funding they receive to "promote democracy") and, above all, the true agents of the Spring events—the emerging secular left, which tried desperately to organize a network of civil society organizations, from trade unions to feminist groups. What further complicates things is the rapidly worsening economic situation, which will sooner or later bring onto the streets millions of the poor—largely absent in the Spring uprisings, which were dominated, initially at least, by educated middle-class youth. This new explosion will *repeat* that of the Spring, forcing it to face its truth, imposing upon political subjects a harsh choice: who is to be the dominant force directing the rage of the poor, translating it into a political program? The new secular left or the Islamists?

The most likely reaction of Western public opinion to the pact between Islamists and the army will no doubt involve a smug display of cynical wisdom. We will be told again and again that, as was already clear in (non-Arab) Iran, popular upheavals in Arab countries always end with the triumph of militant Islamism. Retroactively, Mubarak will then appear as the lesser evil, and the take-home message will be clear—better stick with the devil you know than play around with emancipation. Against this cynical temptation, we should remain unconditionally faithful to the radical emancipatory core of the Egyptian uprising.

CHAPTER SEVEN

Occupy Wall Street, Or, The Violent Silence of a New Beginning

What is to be done in the aftermath of the Occupy Wall Street movement, when the protests that began far away—in the Middle East, Greece, Spain, the UK—reached the center and are now being reinforced and rolling out all around the world? In San Francisco on Sunday October 16, 2011, in an echo of the OWS movement, a man addressed the crowd with an invitation to participate as if it were a happening in the 1960s hippy style: "They are asking us what is our program. We have no program. We are here to have a good time." Such statements reveal one of the great dangers the protesters face: the danger that they will fall in love with themselves, with the fun they are having in the "occupied" zones. But carnivals come cheap—the true test of their worth is what happens the day after, how our everyday life has changed or is to be changed. This requires difficult and patient work—of which the protests are the beginning, not the end. Their basic message is: the taboo has been broken, we do not live in the best possible world; we are allowed, obliged even, to think about the alternatives.

Following a kind of Hegelian triad, the Western left has come full circle: after abandoning so-called "class-struggle essentialism" for the plurality of anti-racist, feminist, and other struggles, "capitalism" is now clearly re-emerging as the name of *the* problem. The first lesson to be learned is not to blame individuals and their attitudes. The problem is not individual corruption or greed, but the system that encourages you to be corrupt. The solution is not "Main Street, not Wall Street," but to change the system in which Main Street is dependent on Wall Street.

Let us then prohibit talk of greed. Public figures from the Pope downwards bombard us with injunctions to resist the culture of excessive greed and consumption, but this spectacle of cheap moralization is an ideological operation if there ever was one. The compulsion (to expand) inscribed into the system itself is here translated into a matter of personal sin, a private psychological propensity. As one theologian close to the Pope put it: "The present crisis is not a crisis of capitalism but a crisis of morality," carefully insinuating that the protesters should be targeting injustice, greed, consumerism, etcetera, rather than capitalism itself. We can congratulate the theologian on his honesty inasmuch as he openly formulates the negation implied in the moralizing critique: the point of emphasizing morality is to prevent the critique of capitalism. The self-propelling circulation of Capital remains more than ever the ultimate Real of our lives, a beast that by definition cannot be controlled. This brings us to our second prohibition: we should reject the simplistic critique of "financial capitalism"—as if there were another "more just" form of capitalism.

But we should also avoid the temptation simply to admire the sublime beauty of uprisings that are doomed to fail. The poetry of failure found its clearest expression in Brecht's note on Mr. Keuner: "'What are you working on?' Mr. K. was asked. Mr. K. replied: 'I'm having a hard time; I'm preparing my next mistake.'"[1] However, this variation on the old Beckettian motif of "fail better" is insufficient: what one should focus on are the results left behind by a failure. For the left today, the problem of "determinate negation" has returned with a vengeance. What new positive order should replace the old one, once the sublime enthusiasm of the uprising has waned? It is here that we encounter the fatal weakness of the current protests. They express an authentic rage that remains unable to transform itself into even a minimal positive program for socio-political change. They express a spirit of revolt without revolution.

Taking a close look at the manifesto of the Spanish *indignados* (the angry ones), for example, throws up some surprises. The first thing that leaps out is the pointedly apolitical tone: "Some of us consider ourselves progressive, others conservative. Some of us are believers,

1   Bertolt Brecht, *Stories of Mr. Keuner*, San Francisco: City Lights 2001, p. 7.

some not. Some of us have clearly defined ideologies, others are apolitical, but we are all concerned and angry about the political, economic, and social outlook which we see around us: corruption among politicians, businessmen, bankers, leaving us helpless, without a voice." They voice their protest on behalf of the "inalienable truths that we should abide by in our society: the right to housing, employment, culture, health, education, political participation, free personal development, and consumer rights for a healthy and happy life." Rejecting violence, they call for an "ethical revolution. Instead of placing money above human beings, we shall put it back to our service. We are people, not products. I am not a product of what I buy, why I buy and who I buy from." It is easy to imagine an honest fascist happily agreeing with all these demands: "placing money above human beings"—yes, this is what Jewish bankers do; "corruption among politicians, businessmen, bankers, leaving us helpless"—yes, we need honest capitalists with the vision to serve their nation, not financial profiteers; "we are people, not products"—yes, we are people whose bond is to the nation, not the market; and so on and so forth. And who will be the agent of this ethical revolution? While the entire political class, right and left, is dismissed as corrupt and driven by a lust for power, the manifesto nonetheless consists of a series of demands addressed to—whom?[2] Not the people themselves: the *indignados* do not (yet) claim that no one will do it for them, that (to paraphrase Gandhi) they themselves have to be the change they want to see.

Reacting to the Paris protests of 1968, Lacan famously said: "What you aspire to as revolutionaries is a new Master. You will get one."[3] It seems that his remark has found its target (not only) in the *indignados*. We got the first glimpse of this new Master in Greece and Italy. As if ironically answering the lack of expert programs offered by the protesters, the trend is now to replace ordinary politicians with a

---

2   During a public debate in Brussels, a member of the *indignados* rejected my critique, arguing that they know precisely what they want: honest and clear political representation in elections, where the left will stand for the real left and the right for the real right. This Confucian strategy of the "rectification of names" is, however, clearly insufficient if the problem is not just the corruption of representative democracy but the "corruption" immanent to the very notion of representative democracy.

3   Jacques Lacan at Vincennes, December 3, 1969: "Ce à quoi vous aspirez comme révolutionnaires, c'est à un Maître. Vous l'aurez."

"neutral" government of depoliticized technocrats (mostly bankers, as in Greece and Italy). Colorful "politicians" are out, grey experts are in. This trend is clearly moving towards a permanent state of emergency and the suspension of political democracy (recall how Brussels reacted to the political events in Greece: with panic at the prospect of a referendum, with relief at the nomination of a new technocrat prime minister). One correlate of this turn to apolitical technocracy is the narrowing of freedom discernible across Europe, including in Turkey, which is gradually emerging as a new model of authoritarian capitalism. A series of ominous signs (such as the arrest in 2011 of over 100 journalists on the ridiculous charge of plotting to overthrow the Islamist government) indicate that economic prosperity and liberalism are covering up the rise of authoritarian Islamism. In other words, Turkey is in reality far from the image, popular in the West, of a country supposed to serve as a model of tolerant political Islam.

Recall a unique incident in 2011, when the Turkish Minister of the Interior Idris Naim Sahin made a speech worthy of a Chestertonian "philosophical policeman." He claimed that the Turkish police were imprisoning thousands of pro-Kurdish BDP members without evidence and without trial, in order *to convince them that they were indeed free prior to their imprisonment.* In Sahin's own words:

> Freedom … What freedom are you talking about when you complain about being imprisoned? If there's no freedom outside the prison, then inside is no different. When you complain about being imprisoned, it means that there's freedom outside. Outside, there's even the freedom to say "I want to divide this country, freedom and autonomy does not suffice, I want to rebel" or whatever. You can't deny this. The only thing you deny is the reality of freedom. You don't accept it, so you deny yourself the freedom to speak about the freedom you enjoy, because your head, your heart, your thoughts are mortgaged … You don't have the freedom to say that the freedoms you enjoy really exist. By destroying you, as well as those who make you talk like this, we are trying to make you free, to free you from the separatists and their extensions. This is what we are doing. It is a very deep, very sophisticated job.[4]

---

4   I owe this reference to Işik Bariş Fidaner, Istanbul.

The madness of this argument is indicative of the "mad" presuppositions of the legal order of power. Its first premise is a simple one: since you claim there is no freedom in our society, you cannot protest when you are deprived of your freedom, since you cannot be deprived of what you do not have. More interesting is the second premise: since the existing legal order is the order of freedom, those who rebel against it are effectively enslaved, unable to accept their freedom—they deprive themselves of the basic freedom to accept the social space of freedom. So, when police arrest you and "destroy" you, they are effectively making you free, freeing you from your self-imposed enslavement. Arresting suspected rebels and torturing them thus becomes "a very deep, very sophisticated job" endowed with metaphysical dignity.

Although this line of reasoning may appear to be based on a rather primitive sophism, it nonetheless contains a grain of truth. There is indeed no freedom outside the social order that, by limiting freedom, creates the space for it. But this grain of truth in fact provides the best argument against it: precisely because the institutional limit to our freedom is the very form of our freedom, it matters a great deal how this limit is structured, what concrete form it takes. The trick of those in power—exemplified by the Turkish philosophical policeman—is to present their form of the limit as the form of freedom as such, so that any struggle against them becomes struggle against society as such.

The situation in Greece looks more promising than it does in Spain, probably due to the recent tradition of progressive self-organization (which disappeared in Spain after the fall of the Franco regime).[5] Even in Greece, however, the protest movement seems to have reached its peak in terms of popular self-organization. The protesters in Syntagma Square maintained a space of egalitarian freedom with no central authority, a public space where all were allotted the same amount of time to speak, and so on. But when they began to debate what to do next, how to move beyond mere protest (should they organize a new political party, for example), the consensus was that what was

---

5 Although right nationalism is also on the rise in Greece, directing its fury at the EU as well as immigrants; and the left echoes this nationalist turn, railing against the EU instead of turning a critical eye on its own past—analyzing, for example, how the government of Andreas Papandreou contributed crucially to the establishment of the Greek "clientelist" state.

needed was not a new party or a direct attempt to take state power, but a civil society movement whose aim would be to exert pressure on the existing political parties. This is clearly inadequate to the task of reorganizing the entirety of social life. To do that, one needs a strong body able to reach quick decisions and realize them with whatever force may be necessary.

It is not enough, then, to reject the depoliticized rule of experts; one must also begin to think seriously about what to propose in place of the predominant economic organization, to imagine and experiment with alternative forms of organization, to search for the germs of the new in the present. Communism is not just or predominantly a carnival of mass protest in which the system is brought to a halt; it is also and above all a new form of organization, discipline, and hard work. Whatever we might say about Lenin, he was fully aware of this urgent need for new forms of discipline and organization.

However, following a properly dialectical necessity, this urge to invent new forms of organization should simultaneously be kept at a distance. What should be resisted at this stage is any hasty translation of the energy of the protest into a set of concrete demands. The protests have created a vacuum—a vacuum in the field of hegemonic ideology, and time is needed to fill this space in a positive fashion. This is why we need not worry too much about the attacks on Occupy Wall Street. The predictable conservative critiques are easy enough to answer. Are the protests un-American? When conservative fundamentalists claim that America is a Christian nation, we should remember what Christianity essentially is: the Holy Spirit, the free egalitarian community of believers united by love. It is the protesters who represent the Holy Spirit, while pagan Wall Street continues to worship false idols (embodied in the statue of the bull). Are the protesters violent? True, their language may appear combative (Occupy!, and so on), but they are violent only in the sense in which Mahatma Gandhi was violent. They are violent insofar as they want to put a brake on the way things are going—but what is this compared to the violence needed to sustain the smooth functioning of the global capitalist system? They are called losers—but are not the true losers those on Wall Street who had to be rescued with hundreds of billions of our dollars? They are called socialists—but in the US, there is already a socialism for the rich. They are accused of not respecting private property—but the

Wall Street speculations that led to the crash of 2008 wiped out more hard-earned private property than anything the protesters would be able to achieve.

The protesters are not communists, if Communism refers to the system which deservedly collapsed in 1990. The only sense in which they are communists is that they care about the commons—the commons of nature, of knowledge—which are threatened by the system. They are dismissed as dreamers, but the real dreamers are those who think that things can go on indefinitely the way they are, with just a few cosmetic adjustments. Far from being dreamers, they are waking from a dream that has turned into a nightmare. They are not destroying anything, but reacting to a system in the process of gradually destroying itself. The protesters are simply calling on those in power to look down into the abyss opening up beneath their feet.

This is the easy part. But the protesters need also beware not only of enemies, but of false friends claiming to support them while working hard to dilute their protest, transforming it into a harmless moralistic gesture. In boxing, to "clinch" means to hold the opponent's body with one or both arms in order to prevent or hinder punches. Bill Clinton's reaction to the Wall Street protests offered a perfect example of political clinching; conceding that the protests were "on balance ... a positive thing," he nevertheless remained worried about the nebulousness of the cause: "They need to be for something specific, and not just against something because if you're just against something, someone else will fill the vacuum you create." Clinton suggested the protesters get behind President Obama's jobs plan, which he claimed would create "a couple million jobs in the next year and a half." But the protesters went out onto the streets because they had had enough of a world in which to recycle your Coke cans, donate a couple of dollars to charity, or buy a Starbucks cappuccino so that 1 percent of the cost goes to the Third World is enough to make people feel good.

The Wall Street protests were thus a beginning, and no doubt one always has to begin this way, with a formal gesture of rejection that is initially more important than any positive content—only such a gesture opens up the space for a new content. In the psychoanalytic sense, the protesters are indeed hysterical actors, provoking the master, undermining his authority; and the question with which they were constantly bombarded, "But what do you want?" aims precisely at precluding the true answer—its point is: "Say it in my terms or shut up!" In this way, the process of translating an inchoate protest into a concrete project is blocked. But the art of politics is also to insist on a particular demand that, while thoroughly "realistic," disturbs the very core of the hegemonic ideology, that is, which, while in principle feasible and legitimate, is de facto impossible (universal healthcare for example). In the aftermath of the Wall Street protests, we should indeed endeavor to mobilize people around such demands—however, it is no less important to remain simultaneously *subtracted* from the pragmatic field of negotiations and "concrete" proposals.

The symbol of Wall Street is the metal statue of a bull in its center—and the standard reactions to the protests indeed mostly took the form of bullshit. In an opinion piece in the *Washington Post*, however, Anne Applebaum proposed a more sophisticated and perfumed version, including references to Monty Python.[6] Since Applebaum's negative version of Clinton's call for more concrete proposals stands for ideology at its purest, it deserves to be quoted in detail. The basis of her reasoning is that the protests around the world were "similar in their lack of focus, in their inchoate nature, and above all in their refusal to engage with existing democratic institutions." She continues:

> In New York, marchers chanted, "This is what democracy looks like," but actually, this isn't what democracy looks like. This is what freedom of speech looks like. Democracy looks a lot more boring. Democracy requires institutions, elections, political parties, rules, laws, a judiciary and many unglamorous, time-consuming activities ... Yet in one sense, the international Occupy movement's failure to produce sound legislative proposals is understandable: both the sources of the global economic crisis and the solutions to it lie, by definition, outside the competence of local and national politicians.

---

6   She makes the acerbic remark that the "human mike" repetition of the speaker's words by the crowd gathered around her is reminiscent of the famous scene from *The Life of Brian* in which the crowd blindly repeats Brian's words "We are all individuals!" This remark is, of course, extremely unfair. Applebaum ignores the fact that the protesters acted like this because they were prohibited by the police from using loudspeakers—the repetition ensured that everyone heard what the speaker had said. One should nonetheless admit that the mechanical repetition soon became a ritual of its own, generating its own *jouissance* whose economy is open to criticism.

The emergence of an international protest movement without a coherent program is therefore not an accident: it reflects a deeper crisis, one without an obvious solution. Democracy is based on the rule of law. Democracy works only within distinct borders and among people who feel themselves to be part of the same nation. A "global community" cannot be a national democracy. And a national democracy cannot command the allegiance of a billion-dollar global hedge fund, with its headquarters in a tax haven and its employees scattered around the world.

Unlike the Egyptians in Tahrir Square, to whom the London and New York protesters openly (and ridiculously) compare themselves, we have democratic institutions in the Western world. They are designed to reflect, at least crudely, the desire for political change within a given nation. But they cannot cope with the desire for global political change, nor can they control things that happen outside their borders. Although I still believe in globalization's economic and spiritual benefits —along with open borders, freedom of movement and free trade— globalization has clearly begun to undermine the legitimacy of Western democracies.

"Global" activists, if they are not careful, will accelerate that decline. Protesters in London shout, "We need to have a process!" Well, they already have a process: It's called the British political system. And if they don't figure out how to use it, they'll simply weaken it further.[7]

The first thing to note is Applebaum's reduction of the Tahrir Square protests to a call for Western-style democracy—once we do this, it of course becomes absurd to compare the Wall Street protests with the Egyptian uprisings: how can protesters here demand what we already have, namely democratic institutions? What is thereby lost from view is the general discontent with the global capitalist system, which obviously takes different forms in different places. But the most shocking part of Applebaum's piece, a truly weird gap in the argument, occurs at the end. After conceding that the undeserved economic consequences of international capitalist finance are beyond the control of democratic mechanisms, which are by definition limited to nation-states, she draws the necessary conclusion that "globalization has

---

7   Anne Applebaum, "What the Occupy Protests Tell Us About the Limits of Democracy," *Washington Post*, October 18, 2011, available at washingtonpost.com.

clearly begun to undermine the legitimacy of Western democracies." So far so good, we might say. This is precisely what the protesters are underlining—that global capitalism undermines democracy. But instead of drawing the only logical conclusion—that we should start thinking about how to expand democracy beyond its state-multiparty form, which has clearly failed to address the destructive consequences of global economic life—she makes an odd about-turn in order to shift the blame onto the protesters themselves, precisely those who began raising these very questions. The last paragraph deserves to be reread carefully: since the global economy is beyond the scope of demo-cratic politics, any attempt to expand democracy in order to embrace it will only accelerate the decline of democracy. What, then, can we do? Re-engage with the existing political system, which, according to Applebaum's own account, is precisely *not* up to the job.

Here we should go all the way to the end. There is no lack of anti-capitalist sentiment today; if anything we are overloaded with critiques of the horrors of capitalism: books, in-depth newspaper investigations, and TV reports abound that investigate companies ruthlessly polluting our environment, corrupt bankers who con-tinue to get fat bonuses while their banks have to be saved by public money, sweatshops where children work overtime, and so on. There is, however, a catch in all this. What as a rule goes unquestioned, ruthless though it may appear, is the democratic-liberal framework as a means of fighting against these excesses. The (explicit or implied) goal is to democratize capitalism, to extend democratic control to the economy, through the pressure of mass media, parliamentary inquiries, stronger regulation, honest police investigations, and so on. But what is never questioned is the democratic institutional framework of the (bour-geois) state of law itself. This remains the sacred cow that even the most radical of these forms of "ethical anti-capitalism" (the Porto Alegre World Social Forum, the post-Seattle movements) do not dare challenge.

It is here that Marx's key insight remains valid, today perhaps more than ever. For Marx, the question of freedom should not be located primarily in the political sphere proper (Does a country have free elections? Are its judges independent? Is the press free from hidden pressures? Are human rights respected? Etcetera). The key to actual freedom rather resides in the network of social relations, from the market to the family, where the kind of change needed if we want genuine improvement is not political reform, but a change in the "apolitical" social relations of production. We do not get to vote on who owns what, or on relations in a factory and so on, for all this is deemed beyond the sphere of the political, and it is illusory to expect that one can actually change things by "extending" democracy to this sphere, by, say, organizing "democratic" banks under the people's control. Radical changes in this domain should be made outside the sphere of legal "rights," etcetera: no matter how radical our anti-capitalism, unless this is understood, the solution sought will involve applying democratic mechanisms (which, of course, can have a positive role to play)—mechanisms, one should never forget, which are themselves part of the apparatus of the "bourgeois" state that guarantees the undisturbed functioning of capitalist reproduction. In this precise sense, Badiou hit the mark with his apparently weird claim that "Today, the enemy is not called Empire or Capital. It's called Democracy."[8] It is the "democratic illusion," the acceptance of democratic procedures as the sole framework for any possible change, that blocks any radical transformation of capitalist relations.

There are thus profound reasons for the present difficulty in formulating a concrete program. But the protesters have drawn attention to two key problems. First, the destructive social consequences of the global capitalist system: hundreds of billions are lost thanks to unbridled financial speculation, and so on. Second, economic globalization is gradually but inexorably undermining the legitimacy of Western democracies. Given their international character, large-scale economic processes cannot be controlled by democratic mechanisms, which are by definition limited to nation-states. For that reason, people increasingly experience democratic institutions as failing in terms of expressing their vital interests. Beneath the profusion of (often confused) statements, the OWS movement thus harbors two basic insights: (1) the contemporary popular discontent is with capitalism *as a system*—the problem is the system as such, not any particular corrupt form of it; (2) the contemporary form of representative multi-party democracy is incapable of dealing with capitalist excesses; in other words, that democracy has to be reinvented. This

---

8   Alain Badiou, "Prefazione all'edizione italiana," in *Metapolitica*, Napoli: Cronopio 2002, p. 14.

brings us to the crux of the issue at stake in the Wall Street protests: how to expand democracy beyond its current political form, which has proved impotent in the face of the destructive consequences of economic life? Is there a name for this reinvented democracy beyond the multi-party representational system? There is indeed: the *dictatorship of the proletariat.*

In a recent book (with a wonderfully convoluted title: *Sarkozy: Worse than Expected / The Others: Expect the Worst*[9]), Badiou proposes an elaborate argument against participation in "democratic" voting: even when an election is effectively "free," and even when one candidate is clearly preferable to another (say, an anti-racist standing against an anti-immigrant populist), one should subtract oneself from voting, since the very *form* of the multi-party election organized by a state is corrupt at a transcendental and formal level. What matters is the formal act of voting, of participating in the process, which signals acceptance of the form itself independently of the particular choice one makes. The exceptions one can make to this universal rule occur at those rare moments when the content (one of the options presented) implicitly undermines the form of voting. Hence one should bear in mind the circular paradox that sustains the "free vote" in our democratic societies: one is free to choose on condition that one makes the right choice—which is why, when the wrong choice is made (as when Ireland rejected the EU constitution, or the Greek prime minister proposed a referendum), it is treated as a mistake, and the establishment immediately imposes a repetition of the vote in order to give the country a chance to correct its error and make the right choice (or, in the case of Greece, simply rejects the proposal itself as representing a false choice).

This is why we should not be afraid to draw the only consistent conclusion from the fact, unsettling for liberal democrats, that the Egyptian Spring has ended (for the time being, since the battle is far from over) with the electoral triumph of the Islamists whose role in the anti-Mubarak revolt of 2011 was negligible: "free elections" or authentic emancipatory revolt—one has to choose. To put it in Rousseau's terms, it was the crowd in Tahrir Square, even though mathematically a minority, that embodied the true *volonté générale*—and, with regard to the Occupy Wall Street movement, it was the small crowd in Zucotti Park which really stood for the "99 percent," and was justified in its distrust of institutionalized democracy.

Of course, the problem remains: how can we institutionalize collective decision-making beyond the framework of the democratic multi-party system? Who will be the agent of this re-invention? Or, to put it in a brutal way: who knows what to do today? There is no Subject who knows, neither in the form of intellectuals nor ordinary people. Is this then a deadlock, a case of the blind leading the blind, or, more precisely, the blind leading the blind where each assumes that the other can see? No, because the respective ignorance is not symmetrical. It is the people who have the answers, they just do not know the questions to which they have (or, rather, are) the answer. John Berger wrote the following about the "multitudes" of those who find themselves on the wrong side of the wall dividing those who are in from those who are out:

> The multitudes have answers to questions which have not yet been posed, and they have the capacity to outlive the walls. The questions are not yet asked because to do so requires words and concepts which ring true, and those currently being used to name events have been rendered meaningless: Democracy, Liberty, Productivity, etc. With new concepts the questions will soon be posed, for history involves precisely such a process of questioning. Soon? Within a generation.[10]

10   John Berger, "Afterword," in Andrey Platonov, *Soul*, New York: New York Review Books 2007, p. 317.

CHAPTER EIGHT

The Wire, Or, What to Do in Non-Evental Times

"**W**ho is David Guetta?" I asked my twelve-year-old son when he triumphantly announced he was going to a Guetta concert. He looked at me as if I were a complete idiot, replying: "Who is Mozart? Google Mozart, you get 5 million hits, google Guetta, you get 20 million!" I did google Guetta and discovered that he is indeed something like a contemporary art curator: not simply a DJ, but an "active" DJ who not only solicits but also mixes and even composes the music he presents, like those curators who no longer only collect works for an exhibition but often directly commission them, explaining to the artists what they want.

And the same goes for David Simon, "curator" of the multitude of directors and screenwriters (including Agnieszka Holland) who collaborated on *The Wire*. The reasons were not simply commercial. The collaboration also represented the nascent form of a new collective process of creation. It is as if the Hegelian *Weltgeist* had recently moved from the cinema to the TV series, although it is still in search of its form. The inner *Gestalt* of *The Wire* is in fact *not* that of a series—Simon himself has referred to *The Wire* as a single sixty-six-hour movie. Furthermore, *The Wire* is not only the result of a collective creative process, but something more: real lawyers, drug addicts, cops, and so on, played themselves; even the names of some characters are condensations of the names of real individuals ("Stringer Bell" is a composite of two real Baltimore drug lords, Stringer Reed and Roland Bell). *The Wire* thus provides a kind of collective self-representation of a city, like the Greek tragedy in which a polis collectively staged its experience.

If *The Wire* is an example of TV realism then, it is less an objective realism (a realistic presentation of a social milieu) than a subjective realism, a film staged by a precisely defined actual social unity. This is signaled by a key scene whose function is precisely to mark its distance from any crude realism, the famous "all-fuck" investigation in Season 1, Episode 4. In an empty ground-floor apartment where a murder has been committed six months previously, detectives McNulty and Bunk, witnessed by a silent housekeeper, try to reconstruct how it happened. But the only word they say during the scene is "fuck" (or variants thereof). They say it 38 times in a row, in so many different ways that it comes to mean just about anything, from annoyed boredom to elated triumph, from pain or shock at the horror of the gruesome murder to pleasant surprise, and it reaches its climax in the self-reflexive reduplication of "Fuckin'fuck!"[1] Imagine the same scene in which each "fuck" is replaced by a more "normal" phrase ("Just another photo!" "Ouch, it hurts!" "Now I get it!" etcetera). The scene works on multiple levels: (1) as a taboo-breaking use of a prohibited word; (2) as a point of seduction (after several hours of "serious stuff," it is designed to function as the moment at which a typical viewer will fall in love with *The Wire*); (3) as a pure phallic joke marking the program's distance from "proper" social-realist drama.

So, once again, what kind of realism are we dealing with here? Let us begin with the title. "Wire" has multiple connotations (walking along a wire, or, of course, the wearing of a wire or bugging device), but the main reference of the title, according to Simon, is "to an almost imaginary but inviolate boundary between the two Americas,"[2] between those participating in the American Dream and those left behind. The topic of *The Wire* is thus the class struggle tout court, the Real of our times, including its cultural consequences. As Fredric Jameson observes: "here, in absolute geographical propinquity, two

---

1   See the detailed analysis by Emmanuel Burdeau in Chapter 1 of Emmanuel Burdeau and Nicolas Vieillescazes, eds., *The Wire: Reconstitution Collective*, Paris: Capricci 2011.

2   Quoted in Tiffany Potter and C. W. Marshall, eds., *The Wire: Urban Decay and American Television*, New York: Continuum 2009, p. 228.

whole cultures exist without contact and without interaction, even without any knowledge of each other: like Harlem and the rest of Manhattan, like the West Bank and the Israeli cities that, once part of it, are now still a few miles away."[3] The two cultures are separated in the basic manner of their relating to the Real: one stands for the horror of addiction and consumption, while in the other, reality is carefully screened.[4] On the horizon, one can even make out the contours of the rich as a new biological race, secured against disease and enhanced through genetic intervention and cloning, while the same technologies are used to control the poor.[5]

Simon is very clear about the concrete historical background of this radical split:

> We pretend to a war against narcotics, but in truth, we are simply brutalizing and dehumanizing an urban underclass that we no longer need as a labor supply … The Wire was not a story about America, it's about the America that got left behind … The drug war is war on the underclass now. That's all it is. It has no other meaning.

This bleak general picture provides the context for Simon's fatalistic worldview: "The Wire is a Greek tragedy in which the postmodern institutions are the Olympian forces. It's the police department, or the

---

3   Fredric Jameson, "Realism and Utopia in The Wire," Criticism, 52: 3–4 (2010), pp. 359–72, available at http://muse.jhu.edu

4   For example, the claim that water-boarding is not torture is obvious nonsense—why, if not by causing pain and fear of imminent death, does it make hardened "terrorists" talk?

5   The premise of Andrew Niccol's movie In Time is that by 2161 genetic alteration has allowed humanity to stop aging at twenty-five, but on reaching that age people are required to earn more time or die within a year. "Living time," which can be transferred among individuals, has replaced money and its availability is displayed on an implant on a person's lower arm: when the clock reaches zero, the person dies instantly. Society is divided by social class into specialized towns called "Time Zones": the rich can live for centuries in luxurious districts, while the poor live in ghettos where youth predominates, and must work each day to earn a few more hours of life, which they must also use to pay for everyday necessities. This dystopian vision of a society in which the expression "time is money" is taken literally, and in which rich and poor are becoming two different races, is emerging as a realistic option with the latest biogenetic developments.

drug economy, or the political structures, or the school administration, or the macroeconomic forces that are throwing the lightning bolts and hitting people in the ass for no decent reason."[6]

Over the last few years, we do indeed seem to have witnessed the rise of a new form of prosopopoeia where the thing which speaks is the market itself, increasingly referred to as if it were a living entity that reacts, warns, makes its opinions clear, etcetera, up to and including demanding sacrifices in the manner of an ancient pagan god. To take just a couple of examples from recent media reports: "When the government announced its measures to combat the deficit, the market reacted cautiously." "The recent fall of the Dow Jones ... signals a clear warning that the market is not so easily satisfied—more sacrifices will be necessary."[7] It may seem that there is an ambiguity as to the precise identity of these "Olympian forces": is it the capitalist market system as such (which is causing the working class to disappear) or the state institutions? Some critics have even proposed reading *The Wire* as a liberal critique of bureaucratic alienation and inefficiency. It is true that a basic (and often described) function of the state bureaucracy is to reproduce itself, not to solve society's problems—even to create problems in order to justify its existence. Recall the famous scene

---

6   All David Simon quotations are from "The Straight Dope: Bill Moyers interviews David Simon," available at www.guernicamag.com.

7   We should, however, resist the temptation to dismiss every such structure of what Jean-Pierre Dupuy calls "self-transcendence" (a system that, although engendered and sustained by the continuous activity of the subjects who participate in it, is necessarily perceived by them as a fixed entity that exists independently of their activity) as a case of "self-alienation" or "reification." True, Dupuy's royal example is that of the market: although we know that the price of a commodity depends on the interaction of millions of participants in the market, each participant treats the price as an objectively imposed independent value. But is not the true example what Lacan calls the "big Other," the symbolic order? Although this order has no objective existence independent of the interaction of subjects engaged in it, each of them has to accomplish a minimal "reification" or "alienation," treating it as an objective determining entity. Far from implying a pathology, this "alienation" is the very measure of normality, that is, of the normativity inscribed into language: in order for any of us to really obey a norm—not spitting in public, say—it is not enough to tell ourselves "the majority does not spit in public"; we have to take a step further and say: "*One* does not spit in public!"—the simple majority of individuals has to be replaced by the minimally "reified" anonymous-impersonal "one."

from Terry Gilliam's *Brazil* in which the hero, who is having problems with his electricity supply, is secretly visited by an illegal electrician (Robert de Niro in a cameo appearance) whose criminality consists of simply repairing the malfunction. The greatest threat to bureaucracy, the most daring conspiracy against its order, comes from those who actually try to solve the problems the bureaucracy is supposed to deal with (like McNulty's group of detectives, who set out actually to break up the drug gang). But does not the same hold for capitalism as such? Its ultimate impetus is likewise not to satisfy existing demands, but to create ever new demands so as to facilitate its continuous expanded reproduction.

It was Marx who formulated early on this idea of the arbitrary and anonymous power of the market as a modern version of Fate. The title of one essay on *The Wire*—"Greek Gods in Baltimore"—is thus quite appropriate: is not *The Wire* the realist counterpart of recent Hollywood blockbusters in which an ancient god or half-god (Perseus in *Percy Jackson*, Thor in *Thor*) finds himself trapped in the body of a confused US adolescent? How is this divine presence felt in *The Wire*? In telling the story of how Fate affects individuals and triumphs over them, *The Wire* proceeds systematically, each successive season taking a further step in the exploration: Season 1 presents the conflict, drug dealers versus police; Season 2 steps back to its ultimate cause: the disintegration of the working class; Season 3 deals with police and political strategies to resolve the problem and their failure; Season 4 shows why education (of black working-class youth) is also insufficient; and, finally, Season 5 focuses on the role of the media: why is the general public not adequately informed of the true scope of the problem? As Jameson has pointed out, the basic procedure of *The Wire* is not to limit itself only to the harsh reality, but to present utopian dreams as part of the world's texture, as constitutive of reality itself. Here are some of the main examples:

In Season 2, Frank Sobotka uses drug-trade money to build up his own contacts, in view of his ultimate project, which is the rebuilding and revitalization of the port of Baltimore: "He understands history and knows that the labor movement and the whole society organized around it cannot continue to exist unless the port comes back. This is then his Utopian project, Utopian even in the stereotypical sense in which it is impractical and improbable—history never moving backwards in this way—and in fact an idle dream that will eventually destroy him and his family."[8]

Also in Season 2, D'Angelo grows more and more ambivalent about the drug trade. When the innocent witness William Gant turns up dead, D'Angelo is shaken, assuming his uncle Avon ordered the killing as revenge for Gant's testimony. D'Angelo is brought in for questioning by McNulty and Bunk who trick him into writing a letter of apology to Gant's family. (In a wonderful Lars von Trier–style manipulation, they show him a photo of two young boys, taken from the desk of a fellow policeman, but presented as photo of Gant's now orphaned sons.) The mob lawyer Levy arrives and stops D'Angelo before he can write anything incriminating, and he is released. Later, having been arrested again, D'Angelo decides to turn state's witness against his uncle's organization; however, a visit from his mother convinces him of his duty to his family, and he backs out of the deal. Because of his refusal to cooperate, he is sentenced to twenty years in prison. Is not the mother who convinces D'Angelo not to testify also mobilizing the family utopia?

In Season 3, Major Colvin conducts a novel experiment: without informing his superiors, he effectively legalizes drugs in West Baltimore, creating a mini Amsterdam, dubbed "Hamsterdam," where the corner dealers are allowed to set up shop. By localizing the drug dealing, which he knows he cannot stop anyway, Colvin eliminates the daily turf battles that drive up the murder rates and dramatically improves daily life for most of his district. Calm returns to terrorized neighborhoods, and his patrolmen, freed from their cars and the endless pursuit of drug-dealing corner boys, return to real police work, walking the beat, getting to know the people they serve. (The real model here is Zurich, not Amsterdam, where back in the 1980s a park behind the main railway station was proclaimed a free zone; there was a similar experiment in Baltimore itself a decade or so ago.)

Also in Season 3, friendship itself is rendered as utopian. Avon and Stringer betray each other, but just before Stringer's murder, the two enjoy one last drink together at Avon's harbor-side condominium, reminiscing about the past and acting as if their old friendship were intact, despite their mutual betrayal. This not simply fakery or hypocrisy, but the expression of a sincere wish for how things might have

8   Jameson, "Realism and Utopia."

been—as John Le Carré put it in *A Perfect Spy*: "Betrayal can only happen if you love."

In Season 4, focused on education, the utopian element is to be found in Pryzbylewski's classroom experiments with computers and his repudiation of the evaluation system imposed by state and federal bodies.

Is not Stringer Bell himself a utopian figure: a pure criminal technocrat, striving to sublate crime into pure business? The underlying ambiguity here is that if these utopias are part of reality, and what makes the world go round, are we then beyond good and evil? In his DVD commentary, Simon points in this direction: "*The Wire* is really not interested in Good and Evil; it's interested in economics, sociology and politics." Jameson is also too hasty in his dismissal of the "outmoded ethical binary of good and evil":

> I have elsewhere argued against this binary system: Nietzsche was perhaps only the most dramatic prophet to have demonstrated that it is little more than an afterimage of that otherness it also seeks to produce—the good is ourselves and the people like us, the evil is other people in their radical difference from us (of whatever type). But society today is one from which, for all kinds of reasons (and probably good ones), difference is vanishing and, along with it, evil itself.[9]

However, this formula seems all too facile. If we discount the premodern (pre-Christian, even) identification of Good with people like us (what about loving one's enemy/neighbor?), is not the properly ethical focus of *The Wire* precisely the problem of the ethical act: what can a (relatively) honest individual do in today's conditions? To put it in Alain Badiou's terms, these conditions (at least a decade ago, when *The Wire* was in the making) were definitely non-evental: there was no potential for a radical emancipatory movement on the horizon. *The Wire* presents a whole panoply of the "types of (relative) honesty," of what to do in such conditions, from McNulty and Colvin up to Lt. Cedric Daniels who, with all his readiness to compromise, sets himself a certain limit (he refuses to meddle with statistics). The key point is that they all have to violate the Law in one way or another. For example, recall how in the final season McNulty aptly manipulates the fact that

9   Ibid.

villainy in mass culture has been reduced to two lone survivors of the category of evil: these two representations of the truly antisocial are, on the one hand, serial killers and, on the other, terrorists (mostly of the religious persuasion, as ethnicity has become identified with religion, and secular political protagonists like the communists and the anarchists no longer seem to be available).[10]

McNulty decides to secure funding for the Marlo Stanfield (the crime boss who takes over after the fall of Avon) investigation by creating the illusion of a serial killer on the loose, in order to draw media attention to the police department. He interferes with crime scenes and falsifies case notes as part of his scheme. However, the basic lesson here is that individual acts are inadequate. A further step is needed, going beyond the individual hero, towards a collective act that, in our present conditions, can only appear as a conspiracy:

> The lonely private detective or committed police officer offers a familiar plot that goes back to romantic heroes and rebels (beginning, I suppose, with Milton's Satan). Here, in this increasingly socialized and collective historical space, it slowly becomes clear that genuine revolt and resistance must take the form of a conspiratorial group, of a true collective … Here Jimmy's own rebelliousness (no respect for authority, alcoholism, sexual infidelities, along with his ineradicable idealism) meets an unlikely set of comrades and co-conspirators—a lesbian police officer, a pair of smart but undependable cops, a lieutenant with a secret in his past but with the hunch that only this unlikely venture can give him advancement, a slow-witted nepotistic appointment who turns out to have a remarkable gift for numbers, various judicial assistants, and finally a quiet and unassuming fixer.[11]

Is not this group a kind of proto-communist cell of conspirators, or a group of eccentrics from a Charles Dickens novel or a Frank Capra film, with the dilapidated basement office they are allocated as their secret conspiratorial lair? G. K. Chesterton's famous formula of law itself as "the greatest and most daring of all conspiracies" here finds an unexpected confirmation. Included in this group of eccentrics, as an informal member from the other side of the divide, is the character

10   Ibid.
11   Ibid.

of Omar Little: Omar's motto can be expressed as the reversal of Brecht's from the *Beggar's Opera*: what is the founding of a bank (as a legal action) compared to robbing a bank?[12] Omar can be placed in the same lineage as the hero of *Dexter*, a series which debuted in 2006. Dexter is a bloodstain-pattern analyst for the Miami police who moonlights as a serial killer. Orphaned at the age of three, he is adopted by Miami police officer Harry Morgan. After discovering the young Dexter's murderous proclivities and to keep Dexter from killing innocent people, Harry begins teaching him "The Code": Dexter's victims must be killers themselves who have killed someone without justifiable cause and will likely do so again. Like Dexter, Omar is also a perfect cop in the guise of its opposite—his code is simple and pragmatic: only kill those who have the authority to order the deaths of others.

But the key figure in *The Wire*'s group of eccentrics is Lester Freamon. Jameson is justified in praising his genius:

> not only to solve … problems in ingenious ways, but also to displace some of the pure mystery and detective interest onto a fascination with construction and physical or engineering problem solving—that is to say, something much closer to handicraft than to abstract deduction. In fact, when first discovered and invited to join the special investigative unit, Freamon is a virtually unemployed officer who spends his spare time making miniature copies of antique furniture (which he sells): it is a parable of the waste of human and intelligence productivity and its displacement—fortunate in this case—onto more trivial activities.[13]

Lester Freamon is the best representative of "useless knowledge"—he is the conspirators' intellectual, rather than an expert, and as such is effective in proposing solutions to actual problems.

---

12 Similarly, the Brechtian lesson in relation to the privatization of the intellectual commons is thus: what is intellectual property theft (piracy) compared to the legal protection of intellectual property? This is why the struggle against the Anti-Counterfeiting Trade Agreement (ACTA) is one of the great emancipatory struggles today. ACTA aims to establish an international legal framework for combating counterfeit goods, generic medicines, and copyright infringement on the internet, and its work should be regulated by a new governing body outside existing forums (another "apolitical" technocratic institution).

13 Jameson, "Realism and Utopia."

So what can this group do? Are they also caught up in a tragic vicious circle in which their very resistance contributes to the system's reproduction? We should bear in mind that there is a key difference between Greek tragedy and the universe of *The Wire*. As Simon himself explains: "Because so much of television is about providing catharsis and redemption and the triumph of character, a drama in which postmodern institutions trump individuality and morality and justice seems different in some ways." In the climactic catharsis of a Greek tragedy the hero encounters his truth and attains sublime greatness in his fall; in *The Wire*, the Big Other of Fate rules in a different way—the system (not life) just goes on, with no cathartic climax.[14]

The consequences of this shift from ancient tragedy to the contemporary form are easy to discern: the absence of narrative closure and of catharsis; the failure of the melodramatic Dickensian benefactor to appear, and so on.[15] The TV series as a *form* also finds its justification in this shift: we never arrive at a final conclusion, not only because we never discover the ultimate culprit (because there is always a new plot behind the current one), but also because the legal system is really striving for its own self-reproduction. This insight is rendered by the final scene of *The Wire*, in which we see McNulty observing the Baltimore port from a bridge, accompanied by a series of flashbacks and glimpses of daily life throughout the city. What we get here is not an ultimate conclusion, but a kind of proto-Hegelian absolute standpoint of reflexive distance, a withdrawal from direct engagement: the idea being that our various struggles, hopes, and defeats are all part of a larger "circle of life" whose true aim is its own self-reproduction, or this very circulation itself. A similar point was made by Marx when he noted that although from the finite subjective standpoint the goal of production is the product—objects that will satisfy people's (imagined or real) needs; use-values in other words—from the absolute standpoint of the system as a totality, the satisfaction of individuals'

---

14   Jon Stewart once remarked that he wished every new US president, upon being elected, was taken to meet five unknown people who would explain how things really work in the US.

15   Is *The Wire* then a "Dickensian" work? Bill Moyers has said that "one day, while screening some episodes of HBO's *The Wire*, it hit me: Dickens was back and his name is David Simon." However, what is missing is precisely the Dickensian melodrama of the last-minute intervention of a kind benefactor.

needs is just a necessary means to keep the machinery of capitalist (re)production going.

The narrative openness of the form is thus grounded in its content. As Jameson puts it, *The Wire* is a whodunit in which the culprit is the social totality, the whole system, not an individual criminal (or group of criminals). But how are we to represent (or, rather, render) in art the totality of contemporary capitalism? In other words, is not totality *always* the ultimate culprit? What is so specific about contemporary tragedy? The point is that the Real of the capitalist system is abstract, the abstract-virtual movement of Capital—here we should mobilize the Lacanian difference between reality and the Real: reality masks the Real. The "desert of the Real" is the abstract movement of capital, and it was in this sense that Marx spoke of "real abstraction." Or, as *The Wire*'s co-producer Ed Burns puts it: "we only allude to the real, the real is too powerful."

Marx described the mad, self-enhancing circuit of capital, whose solipsistic path of self-fecundation reaches its apogee in today's meta-reflexive speculations on futures.[16] It is far too simplistic to claim that the specter of this self-engendering monster pursuing its path without regard for any human or environmental concern is nothing more than an ideological abstraction, and that behind it there are real people and natural objects on whose productive capacities and resources capital's circulation is based and on which it feeds like a gigantic parasite. The problem is not only that this abstraction is part of our financial speculator's misperception of social reality, but that it is also real in the precise sense of determining the structure of material social processes. The fate of whole strata of the population and sometimes of whole countries can be decided by this solipsistic speculative dance of Capital, which pursues its goal of profitability in blessed indifference as to how its movements might affect social reality.

Marx's point was not primarily to reduce this second dimension to the first, or to demonstrate how the theological dance of commodities arises out of the antagonisms of "real life." Rather, his point was

16 The stages in the predominant mode of money seem to obey the Lacanian triad of RSI: gold functions as the Real of money (what it is "really worth"); with paper money we enter the Symbolic register (paper is the symbol of its worth, worthless in itself); and, finally, the emerging mode is a purely "Imaginary" one—money will increasingly exist as a purely virtual point of reference, of accounting, without any actual form, real or symbolic (the "cashless society").

that *one cannot properly grasp the first (the social reality of material production and social interaction) without the second.* It is the self-propelling movement of Capital that runs the show, that provides the key to real-life developments and catastrophes. Therein resides the fundamental systemic violence of capitalism, much more uncanny than any direct pre-capitalist socio-ideological violence. This violence is no longer attributable to individuals and their "evil" intentions, but is purely "objective," systemic, anonymous. Here we encounter the Lacanian difference between reality and the Real: the former is the social reality of actual people involved in interaction and in the productive process, while the Real is the inexorable, "abstract," spectral logic of Capital that determines what goes on in social reality. This gap becomes palpable when one visits a country in which life is obviously in a shambles, marked by ecological decay and human misery, and yet economic reports nonetheless inform us that the country is "financially healthy"—the reality does not matter, what is important is the situation of Capital.

Once again, the question is: what would be the aesthetic correlate of such a Real, what might something like a "realism of abstraction" be?[17] We need a new form of poetry, similar to what Chesterton imagined as a "Copernican poetry":

> It would be an interesting speculation to imagine whether the world will ever develop a Copernican poetry and a Copernican habit of fancy; whether we shall ever speak of "early earth-turn" instead of "early sunrise," and speak indifferently of looking up at the daisies, or looking down on the stars. But if we ever do, there are really a large number of big and fantastic facts awaiting us, worthy to make a new mythology.[18]

At the beginning of Monteverdi's *Orfeo*, the Goddess of Music introduces herself with the words "Io sono la musica..."—is this not something that soon afterwards, when "psychological" subjects invaded the stage, became unthinkable, or rather, unrepresentable? One had to wait until the 1930s for such strange creatures to reappear on the stage. In Brecht's "learning plays," an actor enters the stage and

---

17   I take this expression from Alberto Toscano and Jeff Kinkle, "Baltimore as World and Representation: Cognitive Mapping and Capitalism in *The Wire*," available at http://dossierjournal.com.

18   G. K. Chesteron, *The Defendant*, Dodd, Mead and Co., 1902, p. 50.

addresses the public: "I am a capitalist. I'll now approach a worker and try to deceive him with my talk of the equity of capitalism ..." The charm of this procedure resides in the psychologically "impossible" combination, in one and the same actor, of two distinct roles, as if a person from the play's diegetic reality can also, from time to time, step outside himself and make "objective" comments about his actions and attitudes. This is how one should read Lacan's "*c'est moi, la vérité, qui parle*" from his essay on "*La Chose freudienne*": as the shocking emergence of a word where one would not have expected it—it is the Thing itself that starts to speak.

In a famous passage from *Capital*, Marx resorts to prosopopoeia to bring out the hidden logic of the exchange and circulation of commodities: "If commodities could speak, they would say this: our use-value may interest men, but it does not belong to us as objects. What does belong to us as objects, however, is our value. Our own intercourse as commodities proves it. We relate to each other merely as exchange-values."[19] Can we imagine something like an operatic prosopopoeia: an opera in which commodities themselves sing, rather than the people who exchange them? Maybe this is the only way one could stage *Capital*.

Here we encounter the formal limitation of *The Wire*: it has not solved the formal task of how to render, in a TV narrative, a universe in which abstraction reigns. *The Wire*'s limit is the limit of psychological realism: what is missing in its depiction of objective reality, including its subjective utopian dreams, is the dimension of the "objective dream," of the virtual/Real sphere of Capital. To evoke this dimension, one has to break with psychological realism (perhaps one way is to embrace ridiculous clichés, as do Brecht and Chaplin in their representations of Hitler in *Arturo Ui* and *The Great Dictator*).[20]

The very psychological-realist "concrete" totality that would encompass social reality, including the lived experience of individuals that

19 Karl Marx, *Capital*, Vol. 1, trans. Ben Fowkes, Harmondsworth: Penguin 1976, pp. 176–7.
20 This move beyond psychological realism is clearly signaled by the fact that the symbol of the OWS protesters became the well-known smiling mask (from *V for Vendetta*), which should not be read simply as means of hiding their identity from the police, since it harbors a much more refined insight: the only way to tell the truth is to wear a mask, or, as Lacan put it, the truth has the structure of fiction.

are part of it, is in a more radical sense *abstract*: it abstracts from the gap that separates the Real from its subjective experience. And it is crucial to see the link between this formal limitation of *The Wire* (its remaining within the confines of psychological realism) and, at the level of content, Simon's political limits. His horizon remains that of a "faith in individuals to rebel against rigged systems and exert for dignity." This faith bears witness to Simon's fidelity to the basic premise of the American ideology that postulates the perfectibility of man—in contrast to, say, Brecht, whose motto is "change the system, not individuals": "Mr. Muddle thought highly of man and did not believe that newspapers could be made better, whereas Mr. Keuner did not think very highly of man but did think that newspapers could be made better. 'Everything can be made better,' said Mr. Keuner, 'except man.'"[21]

This tension between institutions and the resistance of individuals limits the political space of *The Wire* to a modest social-democratic individualist reformism: individuals can try to reform the system, but the latter ultimately always wins. What this notion cannot properly grasp is the way these individuals themselves lose their innocence in their struggle—not so much in the sense that they become corrupted, but rather that even if they remain honest and good their acts simply become irrelevant or misfire ridiculously, providing a new impetus to the very force they oppose. We get an intimation of this in *The Wire*'s very first scene, in which McNulty and a black kid commenting on the death of Snot Boogie come across like a Greek chorus:

> McNulty: So your boy's name was what?
> Kid: Snot Boogie.
> McNulty: God. Snot Boogie … This kid, whose mama went to the trouble to christen him Omar Isaiah Betts … You know, he forgets his jacket, his nose starts running and some asshole, instead of giving him a Kleenex, he calls him "Snot." So he's Snot forever. Doesn't seem fair …
> Kid: I'm sayin', every Friday night in an alley behind the Cut Rate, we rollin' bones, you know? I mean all them boys, we roll 'til late.
> McNulty: Alley crap game, right?
> Kid: Like every time, Snot, he'd fade a few shooters, play it out 'til the pot's deep. Snatch and run.
> McNulty: What, every time?

---

21   Bertolt Brecht, *Stories of Mr. Keuner*, San Francisco: City Lights 2001, p. 65.

Kid: Couldn't help hisself.

McNulty: Let me understand. Every Friday night, you and your boys are shootin' craps, right? And every Friday night, your pal Snot Boogie … he'd wait 'til there's cash on the ground and he'd grab it and run away? You let him do that?

Kid: We'd catch him and beat his ass but ain't nobody ever go past that.

McNulty: I've gotta ask you: if every time Snot Boogie would grab the money and run away … why'd you even let him in?

Kid: What?

McNulty: Well, if every time, Snot Boogie stole the money, why'd you let him play?

Kid: Got to. It's America, man.

Here is a tragic vision of a meaningless (life and) death, redeemed only by hopeless resistance—the underlying ethical motto is something like "resist, even if you know that in the end you will lose." Snot (real name Omar) is, of course, a metaphor for the later central character, Omar Little: each time he is beaten, he gets up again and again until he is killed. Not only will you lose, but your death will be a nameless death, like that of Omar Little towards the end of the last season. We see his body in the city's morgue, and all that identifies him now is a name tag, one which was initially misplaced on another body. His murder will remain unaccounted for, he dies without ceremony, with no Antigone demanding his burial. However, this very anonymity of death nonetheless shifts the situation from tragedy to comedy, a comedy harsher than tragedy itself: Snot's death is no tragedy for the same reason that the Holocaust was no tragedy. Tragedy is by definition a tragedy of character, the failure of the hero being grounded in a flaw in his character, but it is obscene to claim that the Holocaust was the result of a Jewish character flaw. The comic dimension is also signaled by the utter arbitrariness of the name: why am I that name? Omar becomes "Snot" for totally external arbitrary reasons. There is no deep reason for his name, in the same way that, in Hitchcock's *North by Northwest*, Roger O. Thornhill is in a totally arbitrary way (mis)identified as "George Kaplan."

But Snot, Omar, McNulty, Lester, and the others, they continue to resist. Later in the first season, McNulty asks Lester why he ruined his career by pursuing a culprit against the orders of the deputy commissioner, and Lester replies that he did it for the same reason

McNulty is now pursuing the Barksdale gang against the wish of his superiors, who merely want some quick street arrests—there is no reason, just the presence of a kind of unconditional ethical drive that links the members of the conspiratorial group. No wonder the series' final scene repeats the beginning: like Snot or Omar, McNulty (along with the others) persists in his Beckettian repeated failure, but this time, finally, the loser is not only beaten, he really loses—loses his job, experiences professional death. McNulty's last line is "Let's go home"—home, that is, outside the public space.

The Wire is often read through the lens of a Foucauldian topos of the relationship between power and resistance, or the law and its transgression: the process of submissive regulation generates what it "represses" and regulates. Recall Foucault's thesis, developed in his *History of Sexuality*, regarding how the medical-pedagogical discourse disciplining sexuality produces the very excess it tries to tame ("sex"), a process begun already in late antiquity when the Christians' detailed descriptions of every possible sexual temptation retroactively generated what they were supposed to suppress. The proliferation of pleasures is thus the obverse of the power that regulates them: power itself generates resistance to itself, the excess it can never control, and the reactions of a sexualized body to its subjection to disciplinary norms are unpredictable. But Foucault here remains ambiguous, shifting the accent (sometimes almost imperceptibly) from *Discipline and Punish* and the first volume of the *History of Sexuality* to the second and third volumes: while in both cases power and resistance are intertwined, Foucault's initial emphasis is on how resistance is appropriated by power in advance, so that power mechanisms dominate the entire field and we become the subjects of power precisely when we resist it. Later, however, the accent shifts to how power generates the excess it cannot control—far from manipulating resistance, power thus becomes unable to control its own effects.

The only way out of this dilemma is to abandon the entire paradigm of "resistance to a *dispositif*": the idea that, while a *dispositif* determines the network of the Self's activity, it simultaneously opens up a space for the subject's "resistance," for its (partial and marginal) undermining and displacement of the *dispositif* itself. The task of emancipatory politics lies elsewhere: not in elaborating a proliferation of strategies of "resisting" the dominant *dispositif* from marginal subjective positions, but in thinking about the modalities of a possible radical rupture in the dominant *dispositif* itself. In all the talk about "sites of resistance" we tend to forget that, difficult as this is to imagine today, from time to time, the very *dispositifs* we resist are themselves subject to change.

This is why, in a profoundly Hegelian way, Catherine Malabou calls on us to abandon the *critical* stance towards reality as the ultimate horizon of our thinking, under whatever name it may appear, from the Young Hegelian "critical critique" to twentieth-century Critical Theory.[22] What such a critical stance has failed to accomplish is the fulfillment of its own gesture: the radicalization of the subjective negative-critical attitude towards reality in a full critical self-negation. Even if it means exposing oneself to the accusation of "regressing" to the Old Hegelian position, we should adopt the authentically Hegelian *absolute* position that, as Malabou points out, involves a kind of speculative "surrender" of the Self to the Absolute, a kind of *absolution*, or release from engagement, albeit in a Hegelian-dialectical way—that is, not an immersion of the subject into the higher unity of an all-encompassing Absolute, but the inscription of the "critical" gap that separates the subject from the (social) substance it resists into this substance itself, as its own antagonism or self-distance.

The reflexive withdrawal rendered in the very last scene of *The Wire* stands for precisely such a "surrender to the Absolute." Here this gesture refers specifically to the relationship between the law and its violations. From the "absolute standpoint," it becomes clear that the (legal) system not only tolerates illegality, but indeed requires it, since it is a condition of the system's own ability to function. From my military service (in 1975, in the infamous Yugoslav People's Army), I remember how, during a class on law and patriotic values, the instructing officer solemnly declared that international regulations prohibit shooting at a paratrooper while he is still in the air; in the next class, on how to use a rifle, the same officer explained how to aim at a paratrooper in the air (taking into account the velocity of his fall and thus aiming a little bit lower, etcetera). Somewhat naively, I asked the officer whether there was not a contradiction between what he was now saying and what he had said an hour earlier; he gave me a look

---

22   See Judith Butler and Catherine Malabou, *Sois mon corps: Une lecture contemporaine de la domination et de la servitude chez Hegel*, Paris: Bayard 2010.

full of scorn as if to say, "How can anyone be so utterly stupid as to ask such a question?" More generally, it is well known that most "Socialist" states were able to function only by relying on the black market (which provided, among other things, 30 percent of the food available)—had one of the regular official campaigns against this network succeeded, the whole system would have collapsed.

In the world of *The Wire*, the crucial question with regard to this relationship between the legal order and its transgression does not concern the status of drug dealing, etcetera, since it is clear that the legal system itself generates much of the crime it fights. The central question is more insidious and unsettling: what is the status of the (utopian) acts of resistance portrayed? Are they also merely a moment in the totality of the system? Are the individual acts of resistance on the part of Snot and Omar, Freamon and McNulty, also just the obverse of the system that ultimately sustains them? If so, then the answer is obvious, if counterintuitive: the only way to stop the system from working is to stop resisting it.

Here a (perhaps surprising) detour through the novels of Ayn Rand may help us to clarify the point. The true conflict in the universe of Rand's two novels is not that between the prime movers and the crowd of second-handers who depend on the prime movers' productive genius—with the tension between the prime mover and his feminine sexual partner being a mere sub-plot of this principal conflict. Rather, the true conflict is between the prime movers themselves, in the (sexualized) tension between the prime mover, the being of pure drive, and his hysterical partner, the potential prime mover who remains caught up in a deadly self-destructive dialectic (between Roark and Dominique in *The Fountainhead*, between John Galt and Dagny in *Atlas Shrugged*). When, in *Atlas Shrugged*, one of the prime-mover figures tells Dagny that the prime movers' true enemy is not the crowd of second-handers but Dagny herself, this is to be taken literally. And Dagny is aware of it: when prime movers start to disappear from public life, she suspects a dark conspiracy, a "destroyer" who is forcing them to withdraw and will thus gradually bring all of social life to a standstill. What she does not yet see is that the figure of the "destroyer" she identifies as the ultimate enemy is the figure of her true Redeemer. The solution comes when the hysterical subject finally escapes her enslavement and recognizes the "destroyer" as her savior.

But why? Second-handers possess no ontological consistency of their own, which is why the key to finding the solution is not to break them, but to break the chain that forces the creative prime movers to work for them. When this chain is broken, the second-handers' power will dissolve by itself. The chain that links a prime mover to the perverted existing order is none other than her attachment to her productive genius: a prime mover is ready to pay any price, up to and including the utter humiliation of feeding the very force that works against her, just to be able to continue to create.

What the hystericized prime mover must embrace is thus a fundamental existential indifference: she must no longer be willing to remain hostage to the second-handers' blackmail, she must be ready to give up the very kernel of her being, that which means everything to her, and accept the "end of the world," the (temporary) suspension of the very flow of energy that keeps the world running. In order to gain everything, she must be ready to go to the zero-point of losing everything.[23]

Mutatis mutandis, exactly the same goes for *The Wire*: in order to make the step from reformism to radical change, we must pass through the zero-point of abstaining from acts of resistance which only keep the system alive. In a strange kind of release, we have to cease to worry about other people's worries, and withdraw into the role of a passive observer of the system's circular self-destructive movement. For example, in relation to the ongoing financial crisis that threatens the euro and other currencies, we should stop worrying about how to prevent financial collapse in order to keep the whole system going. The model for such a stance is Lenin during World War I: ignoring all "patriotic" worries about the motherland in danger, he coolly steps back to observe the deadly imperialist dance while laying the foundations for the future revolutionary process—his worries were not the worries of most of his countrymen.

---

23 We can imagine a strike conducted, not by the Randian mythic "achievers," but by what one can call the "inherent transgressors": those who, in "resisting" the system and transgressing its rules effectively make it viable. Imagine the black marketeers in today's Cuba suspending their activity: arguably the economic system would collapse in weeks. Something similar occurs in Western countries as the "work to rule" strike: when state employees in a sensitive branch, like the customs or health services, simply follow the rules to the letter, thereby bringing the system virtually to a halt.

As was clear to Rand, if we want to see real change, then our own worries and cares are our main enemy. We need to stop fighting small battles against the inertia of the system, attempting to make things better here and there, and instead prepare the terrain for the big battle to come. The standpoint of the Absolute is simple enough to achieve; one merely has to withdraw to the (usually aestheticized) position of totality, as in the popular song the "Circle of Life" from *The Lion King* (words by Tim Rice):

> It's the Circle of Life
> And it moves us all
> Through despair and hope
> Through faith and love
> Till we find our place
> On the path unwinding
> In the Circle
> The Circle of Life

The song is sung by, of course, the lions: life is a great circle, we eat the zebras, the zebras eat grass; but then, after we die and return to the earth, we also feed the grass, and the circle is closed—this is the best message imaginable for those at the top. The crucial thing is the political spin we give to such "wisdom": is it a matter of simple withdrawal or of withdrawal as the condition for a radical act?[24] In other words, yes, life always forms a circle, but it is still possible (sometimes) not just to climb or descend its hierarchy, but to change the circle itself. Here we should indeed follow Christ, as the paradox of the Absolute itself renouncing the standpoint of the Absolute and adopting the radically "critical" stance of a finite agent engaged in a terrestrial struggle. This stance is deeply Hegelian, Hegel's main thesis being precisely that of an Absolute strong enough to "finitize" itself, to act as a finite subject.

In other words, reflexive withdrawal into the standpoint of the Absolute does not entail a retreat into inactivity, but the opening up of

---

24   Can we imagine a slight change to the film *Life Is Beautiful*, with the father singing a similar song to the son? "The Nazis are killing us here in Auschwitz, but you should see, my son, how all this is part of a larger Circle of Life: the Nazis themselves will die and turn into fertilizer for the grass, which will be eaten by the cows; the cows will be slaughtered and we will eat their meat in our pies."

a space for radical change. The point is not to resist Fate (and thus only aid its accomplishment—like the parents of Oedipus and the servant from Baghdad who fled to Samara), but to change Fate itself, its basic coordinates. Jean-Luc Godard once proposed the motto "*Ne change rien pour que tout soit différent*" (change nothing so that everything will be different), a reversal of "some things must change so that everything remains the same." In some political constellations, such as the late capitalist dynamic that requires constant self-revolutionizing to maintain the system, those who refuse to change anything are effectively the agents of true change: effecting a change in the very principle of change.

Therein resides the ambiguity of *The Wire*'s finale: does it suggest a resigned and tragic form of wisdom or the opening up of a space for a more radical act? This ambiguity clouds the bright vision of *The Wire* as "a Marxist's dream of a series" (as one sympathetic leftist critic dubbed it). Simon himself is clear here. When asked if he was a socialist, he declared himself a social democrat who believes that capitalism is the only game in town: "you're not looking at a Marxist here ... I accept that [capitalism] is the only viable way to generate wealth on a large scale." But does not his own tragic worldview contradict this reformist social-democratic vision? While putting his faith in rebellious individuals, he is nevertheless

> doubtful that the institutions of a capital-obsessed oligarchy will reform themselves short of outright economic depression (New Deal, the rise of collective bargaining) or systemic moral failure that actually threatens middle-class lives (Vietnam and the resulting, though brief commitment to rethinking our brutal foreign-policy footprints around the world).

Are we not today approaching an "outright economic depression"? Will such a prospect give rise to a properly collective counter-institution?[25] Whatever the outcome, one thing is clear: only when we fully embrace Simon's tragic pessimism, accepting that there is no future (within the system), can an opening emerge for a radical change to come.

---

25 I rely here on Kieran Aarons and Grégoire Chamayou, Chapter 3 of *The Wire: Reconstitution Collective*, pp. 86–7.

CHAPTER NINE

Beyond Envy and Resentment

As a solution to what one is tempted to call the "antinomies of the Welfare State," the strange thing about Peter Sloterdijk's attempt to develop an "ethics of gift-giving"[1] beyond mere market exchange is that it brings us unexpectedly close to the Communist vision. Sloterdijk is guided by the elementary lesson of dialectics: sometimes, the opposition between keeping things as they are and changing them does not cover the entire field, that is, sometimes, the only way to maintain what is worth keeping in the old is to intervene and change things radically. If, today, one wants to save the core of the welfare state, one should precisely abandon any nostalgia for twentieth-century social democracy. What Sloterdijk proposes is a new kind of cultural revolution, a radical psycho-social transformation based on the insight that, today, the exploited productive stratum is no longer the working class, but the (upper-)middle class: they are the true "givers" whose heavy taxation finances the education, health, etcetera, of the majority. In order to accomplish this change, we should leave behind the current *étatisme*, this absolutist remainder, which has strangely survived in our democratic era: the idea, surprisingly strong even on the traditional left, that the state has the unquestionable right to tax its citizens, to determine and seize through legal coercion (if necessary) part of their product. It is not that citizens give part of their income to the state—they are treated as if they are a priori indebted to the state. This attitude is sustained by a misanthropic premise that is strong-

---

1   See Peter Sloterdijk, *Repenser l'impot*, Paris: Libella 2012.

est among the very left that otherwise preaches solidarity: people are basically egotists, so they have to be forced to contribute something to the common welfare, and it is only the state that, by means of its coercive apparatus, can do the job of assuring the necessary solidarity and redistribution.

According to Sloterdijk, the ultimate cause of this weird social perversion is an imbalance between eros and thymos, between the possessive erotic drive to amass things and the drive (predominant in premodern societies) to pride and generosity, to a giving that brings respect. The best way to reestablish this balance is to give full recognition to thymos: to treat those productive of wealth not as a group that is a priori suspicious for refusing to pay its debt to society, but as the true givers whose contribution should be fully recognized, so that they can be proud of their generosity. The first step is to make the shift from proletariat to volontariat. Instead of taxing the rich excessively, one should give them the (legal) right to decide voluntarily what part of their wealth they will donate to the common welfare. To begin with, of course, this does not mean radically lowering taxes, but simply opening up at least a small domain in which the givers are given the freedom to decide how much they will donate and to what—such a beginning, modest as it is, would gradually change the entire ethics on which social cohesion is based.

Are we not caught here in the old paradox of freely choosing what we are any way obliged to do? That is to say, is it not the case that the freedom of choice accorded to the "voluntariat" of "achievers" is a false freedom that relies on a forced choice? Are not the "achievers" free to choose (whether to give money to society or not) only if they make the right choice? There is a series of problems with this idea—but they are not those identified by the (predictable) leftist outcry against Sloterdijk. First, who, in our societies, really are the givers (the achievers)? Let us not forget that the 2008 financial crisis was caused by the rich givers/achievers, and the "ordinary people" financed the state to bail them out. (Exemplary here is Bernard Madoff, who first stole billions and then played the giver, donating millions to charities, etcetera) Second, getting rich does not happen in a space outside the state and community, but involves (as a rule) a violent process of appropriation that casts serious doubt on the right of the rich achiever to own the wealth he may then go on to give generously. Last but not least, Sloterdijk's opposition of possessive eros and giving thymos is all too simplistic: is authentic erotic love not giving at its purest? (Remember Juliet's famous lines: "My bounty is as boundless as the sea, / My love as deep; the more I give to thee, / The more I have, for both are infinite.") And cannot thymos also be destructive? One should always bear in mind that envy (resentment) is a case of thymos intervening in the domain of eros, distorting "normal" egotism, making what the other has (and I don't have) more important than what I have. More generally, the basic reproach to Sloterdijk should be: why do you champion generosity only within the constraints of capitalism, which is *the* order of possessive eros and competition? Within these constraints, every generosity is a priori reduced to being the obverse of brutal possessiveness, a benevolent Dr. Jekyll to the capitalist Mr. Hyde. We need only recall the first model of generosity mentioned by Sloterdijk, Andrew Carnegie, the man of steel with a heart of gold, as they say. After using Pinkerton detective agents and a private army to crush workers' resistance, he displayed his generosity by (partially) giving back what he had (not created but) grabbed. Even with Bill Gates, how can one forget the brutal tactics he employed to crush competitors and secure a monopoly? The key question is thus: is there no place for generosity outside the capitalist frame? Is each and every such project a case of sentimental moralistic ideology?

We often hear it said that the Communist vision relies on a dangerous idealization of human beings, attributing to them a kind of "natural goodness" that is simply alien to our (egotist, etcetera) nature. However, in his book *Drive*,[2] Daniel Pink refers to a body of behavioral science research that suggests, sometimes at least, external incentives (money rewards) can be counterproductive: optimal performance comes when people find intrinsic meaning in their work. Incentives may be useful in getting people to accomplish boring routine work; but with more intellectually demanding tasks, the success of individuals and organizations increasingly depends on being nimble and innovative, so there is a greater need for people to find intrinsic value in their work. Pink identifies three elements underlying such motivation: autonomy, the ability to choose what and how tasks are completed; mastery, the process of becoming adept at an activity; and

---

2   See Daniel H. Pink, *Drive: The Surprising Truth About What Motivates Us*, New York: Riverhead Books 2009.

purpose, the desire to improve the world. Here is the transcript of a report on a study conducted at MIT:

> They took a whole group of students and they gave them a set of challenges. Things like memorizing strings of digits, solving word puzzles, other kinds of spatial puzzles, even physical tasks like throwing a ball through a hoop. To incentivize their performance they gave them three levels of rewards: if you did pretty well, you got a small monetary reward; if you did medium well, you got a medium monetary reward; if you did really well, if you were one of the top performers you got a large cash prize. Here's what they found out. As long as the task involved only mechanical skill bonuses worked as they would be expected, the higher the pay, the better their performance. But once the task calls for even rudimentary cognitive skill a larger reward led to poorer performance. How can that possibly be? This conclusion seems contrary to what a lot of us learned in economics, which is that the higher the reward, the better the performance. And they're saying that once you get above rudimentary cognitive skill it's the other way around, which seems like the idea that these rewards don't work that way, seems vaguely Left-Wing and Socialist, doesn't it? It's this kind of weird Socialist conspiracy. For those of you who have these conspiracy theories I want to point out the notoriously left-wing socialist group that financed the research: the Federal Reserve Bank. Maybe that 50 dollar or 60 dollar prize isn't sufficiently motivating for an MIT student—so they went to Madurai in rural India, where 50 or 60 dollars is a significant sum of money. They replicated the experiment in India and what happened was that the people offered the medium reward did no better than the people offered the small reward but this time around, the people offered the top reward they did worst of all: higher incentives led to worse performance. This experiment has been replicated over and over and over again by psychologists, by sociologists and by economists: for simple, straightforward tasks, those kinds of incentives work, but when the task requires some conceptual, creative thinking those kind of motivators demonstrably don't work. The best use of money as a motivator is to pay people enough to take the issue of money off the table. Pay people enough, so they are not thinking about money and they're thinking about the work. You get a bunch of people who are doing highly skilled work but they're willing to do it for free and volunteer their time 20, sometimes 30 hours a week; and what they create, they give it away, rather than sell it. Why are these people, many of whom are technically

sophisticated highly skilled people who have jobs, doing equally, if not more, technically sophisticated work not for their employer, but for someone else for free! That's a strange economic behavior.[3]

This "strange behavior" is that of a communist following Marx's well-known motto "From each according to his abilities, to each according to his needs"—*this* is the only ethics of gift-giving that has any authentic utopian dimension. "Postmodern" capitalism is, of course, very apt at exploiting these elements for its own profitability— not to mention the fact that, behind every "postmodern" company allowing its employees the space for "creative" achievement, there is the anonymous old-fashioned working-class exploitation. The icon of today's creative capitalism is Apple—but what would Apple be without Foxconn, the Taiwanese company that owns large factories in China where hundreds of thousands assemble iPads and iPods in abominable working conditions? We should not forget the obverse of the postmodern "creative" center in Silicon Valley, where a couple of thousand researchers engage in testing new ideas: the militarized barracks in China plagued by a series of worker suicides, as a result of stressful conditions (long hours, low pay, high pressure). After the eleventh worker had jumped to his death, the company introduced a series of measures compelling workers to sign contracts promising not to kill themselves, to report fellow workers who appeared depressed, to go to psychiatric institutions if their mental health deteriorated, etcetera.[4] To add insult to injury, Foxconn began to put up safety nets around the buildings of its vast factory. (No wonder Terry Gou, the chairman of Hon Hai [the parent company of Foxconn], referred to his employees as animals at an end-of-year party, complaining that "to manage one million animals gives me a headache." Gou added that he wanted to learn from Chin Shih-chien, the director of the Taipei Zoo, exactly how animals should be "managed," and invited the zoo director to speak at Hon Hai's annual review meeting, urging his general managers to listen carefully.[5])

Whatever the problems with experiments such as the one at MIT, they definitely demonstrate that there is nothing "natural" about

---

3   Cited from Dan Pink, "Transcript for RSA Animate—Drive: The surprising truth about what motivates us," available at http://dotsub.com.

4   "Foxconn Ups Anti-suicide Drive," www.straitstimes.com.

5   "Foxconn Chief Calls Employees 'animals,'" www.examiner.com.

capitalist competition and profit-maximizing. Above a certain level of satisfying basic needs, people tend to behave in what one cannot but call a communist way, giving to society according to their abilities, not according to the financial remuneration they get. Which brings us back to Sloterdijk and his celebration of the donations of rich capitalists as displaying a "neo-aristocratic pride"—but how about contrasting this with what Badiou once referred to as "proletarian aristocratism"? This is why, in the domain of literature, there are important examples of anti-bourgeois aristocrats who finally come to understand that the only way they can retain their pride is by joining the other side, in opposition to the bourgeois way of life. Surprisingly perhaps, even a figure like Shakespeare's Coriolanus can be reappropriated for emancipatory politics in this way.

Marx noted apropos of Homer how "the difficulty lies not in understanding that the Greek arts and epic are bound up with certain forms of social development. The difficulty is that they still afford us artistic pleasure and that in a certain respect they count as a norm and as an unattainable model."[6] The way to test a really great work of art is to ask how well it survives de-contextualization, its transposition into a new context. Perhaps the best definition of a classic is that it functions like the eyes of God in an Orthodox icon: no matter where you stand in the room, they seem to look specifically at you. No wonder that by far the best cinema version of Dostoyevsky is Kurosawa's *Idiot* set in Japan after World War II, with Myshkin as a returning soldier. The point is not simply that we are dealing with an eternal conflict that appears in all societies, but a much more precise one: with each new context, a classic work of art seems to address the very specific quality of each epoch—this is what Hegel called "concrete universality." There is a long history of such successful transpositions of Shakespeare—to mention just a few recent film versions: *Othello* in a contemporary jazz club (Basil Dearden's *All Night Long*, 1962); *Richard III* in an imagined Fascist UK of 1930s (Richard Loncraine, 1995); Baz Luhrmann's *Romeo + Juliet* in Venice Beach, California (1996); *Hamlet* in corporate New York (Michael Almereyda, 2000).

Coriolanus poses a special challenge to such re-contextualization. The play is so exclusively focused on its hero's militaristic and

---

6   Karl Marx, *Grundrisse*, trans. Martin Nicolaus, Harmondsworth: Penguin 1973, p. 111.

aristocratic pride and his contempt for ordinary people that one can easily see why, after the German defeat in 1945, the allied occupation authorities prohibited its performance on account of its anti-democratic message. Consequently, the play seems to offer a rather narrow interpretive choice. That is to say, what are the alternatives to staging the play the way it is, surrendering to its militaristic anti-democratic lure? We can try to subtly "extraneate" this lure by way of its excessive aestheticization; we can do what Brecht did in his rewriting of it, shifting the focus from the display of emotions (Coriolanus's rage, etcetera) to the underlying conflict of political and economic interests (in Brecht's version, the crowd and the tribunes are not driven by fear and envy, but act rationally in view of their situation); or, perhaps the worst choice, we can engage in some pseudo-Freudian stuff about the maternal fixation of Coriolanus and the homosexual intensity of the relationship between Coriolanus and Aufidius.

Ralph Fiennes (along with his scenario writer John Logan) did the impossible with his 2011 movie version, thereby perhaps confirming T. S. Eliot's famous claim that *Coriolanus* is superior to *Hamlet*: he broke out of this closed circle of interpretive options, all of which introduce a critical distance towards the figure of Coriolanus, and *fully asserted* Coriolanus—not as a fanatical anti-democrat, but as a figure of the radical left. Fiennes's first move was to change the geopolitical coordinates of *Coriolanus*: Rome is now a contemporary colonial city-state in crisis and decay, and the Volscians are leftist guerilla rebels organized in what we call today a rogue state. (Think of Colombia and FARC, the "revolutionary armed forces of Colombia" holding a vast territory in the south of the country—if FARC were not corrupted by drug-dealing.) This first move includes many perspicuous details, such as the decision to present the borderline between the territory held by the Roman army and the rebel territory, the place of contact between the two sides, as a lone access ramp on a highway, a kind of guerilla checkpoint. (One can dream further here: what about fully exploiting the fact that the film was shot in Serbia, with Belgrade as "a city that called itself Rome," and imagining the Volscians as Albanians from Kosovo, with Coriolanus as a Serb general who changes sides and joins the Albanians?)

The choice of Gerard Butler for the role of Aufidius, the Volscian leader and Caius Martius's (Coriolanus's) opponent, was a particularly good one. Since Butler's greatest hit was Zack Snyder's *300*, in which he played Leonidas, we should not be afraid to venture the hypothesis that, in both films, he basically plays the same role: the warrior-leader of a rogue-state fighting a mighty empire. *300*, the saga of the 300 Spartan soldiers who sacrificed themselves at Thermopylae to halt the invasion of Xerxes' Persian army, was attacked as the worst example of patriotic militarism with clear allusions to the recent tensions with Iran and events in Iraq. Are things really so clear, however? The film should rather be vehemently defended against these accusations. It is the story of a poor small country (Greece) invaded by the army of a much larger state (Persia), at that point much more developed and with a much more advanced military technology. Are not the Persian elephants, giants, and large fire arrows the ancient version of high-tech weaponry? When the last surviving group of Spartans and their king Leonidas are killed by thousands of arrows, are they not in a way bombed to death by techno-soldiers operating sophisticated weapons from a safe distance, like today's US soldiers firing rockets from warships in the Persian Gulf?

Furthermore, Xerxes' words when he attempts to convince Leonidas to accept Persian domination definitely do not sound like the words of a fanatical Muslim fundamentalist. He tries to seduce Leonidas into subjection by promising him peace and sensual pleasure if he rejoins the Persian global empire. All he asks from him is a formal gesture of kneeling down, of recognizing the Persian supremacy—if the Spartans do this, they will be given supreme authority over the whole of Greece. Is this not essentially what President Reagan demanded from the Nicaraguan Sandinista government? That they should just say "Uncle!" to the US... And is not Xerxes' court depicted as a kind of multiculturalist, multi-lifestyle paradise? In this case then, the Spartans, with their discipline and spirit of self-sacrifice, are more like the Taliban defending Afghanistan against the US occupation (or the elite units of the Iranian Revolutionary Guard, ready to sacrifice themselves in the event of an American invasion). Perspicuous historians have already noted the parallel. Here is the cover text for Tom Holland's *Persian Fire*: "In the fifth-century BC, a global superpower was determined to bring truth and order to what it regarded as two terrorist states. The superpower was Persia, incomparably rich in ambition, gold and men. The terrorist states were Athens and Sparta, eccentric cities in a poor and mountainous backwater: Greece."[7]

A programmatic statement towards the end of *300* defines the Greeks' agenda as "against the reign of mystique and tyranny, towards the bright future," further specified as the rule of freedom and reason—it sounds like an elementary Enlightenment program, with a Communist twist even! Recall also that, at the film's beginning, Leonidas rejects outright the message of the corrupt "oracles," according to whom the gods forbid the military expedition to stop the Persians—as we later learn, the "oracles," who were allegedly receiving a divine message in an ecstatic trance, were effectively being paid by the Persians, just like the Tibetan "oracle" who in 1959 delivered to the Dalai Lama the message to leave Tibet but who was—as we now know—on the payroll of the CIA.

But what about the apparent absurdity of the Spartan idea of dignity, freedom, and Reason, sustained by extreme military discipline, including the practice of discarding weak children? This "absurdity" is simply the price of freedom—freedom is not free, as they put it in the film. Freedom is not something given, it is gained through a hard struggle in which one must be ready to risk everything. The Spartans' ruthless discipline is not simply the external opposite of Athenian "liberal democracy," it is its inherent condition, what lays the foundation for it: the free subject of Reason can only emerge through ruthless self-discipline. True freedom is not a freedom of choice made from a safe distance, like choosing between strawberry cake or chocolate cake; true freedom overlaps with necessity, a truly free choice involves putting one's very existence at stake—choosing because one simply "cannot do otherwise." If one's country is under foreign occupation and one is called upon to join the resistance, the reason given is not "You are free to choose," but "Can't you see that this is the only thing you can do if you want to retain your dignity?" No wonder all early modern egalitarian radicals, from Rousseau to the Jacobins, admired the Spartans and imagined Republican France as a new Sparta: there is an emancipatory core in the Spartan spirit of military discipline that survives even when we subtract all the historical paraphernalia of class rule, the ruthless exploitation of slaves, etcetera—no wonder Trotsky

---

7   Tom Holland, *Persian Fire*, New York: Doubleday 2006.

called the Soviet Union in the difficult years of "war communism" "proletarian Sparta."

Soldiers are not bad per se—what is bad are soldiers inspired by *poets*, soldiers mobilized by nationalist poetry. This, finally, brings us back to *Coriolanus*. Who is the poet there? Before Caius Martius (Coriolanus) enters the stage, it is Menenius Agrippa who pacifies the furious crowd demanding grain. Like Ulysses in *Troilus and Cressida*, Menenius is the ideologist par excellence, offering a poetic metaphor to justify social hierarchy (in this case, the rule of the senate); and, in the best corporatist tradition, the metaphor is that of a human body. Here is how Plutarch, in his "Life of Coriolanus," retells this story first reported by Livy:

> It once happened that all the other members of a man mutinied against the stomach, which they accused as the only idle, uncontributing part the whole body, while the rest were put to hardships and the expense of much labor to supply and minister to its appetites. The stomach, however, merely ridiculed the silliness of the members, who appeared not to be aware that the stomach certainly does receive the general nourishment, but only to return it again, and redistribute it amongst the rest. Such is the case, ye citizens, between you and the senate. The counsels and plans that are there duly digested, convey and secure to all of you your proper benefit and support.[8]

How does Coriolanus relate to this metaphor of the body and its organs, of the rebellion of the organs against their body? It is clear that, whatever Coriolanus is, he does not stand for the body, but is an organ that not only rebels against the body (the body politic of Rome), but abandons it by going into exile—a true *organ without a body*. Is Coriolanus then really against the people? *Which* people? The plebeians represented by the two tribunes, Brutus and Sicinius, are not exploited workers, but rather a lumpenproletarian mob, the rabble fed by the state; and the two tribunes are their proto-fascist manipulators—to quote Kane (the citizen from Welles's film), they speak for the poor *so that the poor will not speak for themselves*. If one looks for the "people," they are rather to be found among the Volscians. Look closely at how Fiennes depicts their capital: a modest popular city

---

8   Plutarch, *Lives of Illustrious Men*, Bedford: Clarke and Company 1887, p. 350.

in a liberated territory, with Aufidius and his comrades in the uniforms of guerilla fighters mixing freely with the common people in an atmosphere of relaxed festivity, in clear contrast to the stiff formality of Rome.

So yes, Coriolanus is a killing machine, a "perfect soldier"; but precisely as such, as an "organ without a body," he has no fixed class allegiance and can easily put himself in the service of the oppressed—as was made clear by Che Guevara, a revolutionary also has to be a killing machine: "Hatred as an element of struggle; a relentless hatred of the enemy impelling us over and beyond the natural limitations that man is heir to and transforming him into an effective, violent, selective, and cold killing machine. Our soldiers must be thus; a people without hatred cannot vanquish a brutal enemy."[9]

There are two scenes in the film that provide a clue for such a reading. When, after his violent outburst in the senate, Coriolanus exits the hall slamming the doors behind him, he finds himself in the silence of a large corridor confronted with an old tired cleaning man, and the two exchange glances in a moment of silent solidarity, as if only the poor cleaner can see who Coriolanus is now. The other scene is a long depiction of his voyage into exile, road-movie style, with Coriolanus as a lone rambler on a trek, anonymous among the ordinary people. It is as if Coriolanus, obviously out of place in the delicate hierarchy of Rome, only now becomes what he is, gains his freedom—and the only thing he can do to retain his freedom is join the Volscians. He does so not simply in order to take revenge on Rome; he joins them because he belongs there—it is only among the Volscian fighters that he can be what he is. Coriolanus's pride is authentic, together with his reluctance to be praised by his compatriots or to engage in political maneuvering—such a pride has no place in Rome, it can thrive only among the guerilla fighters.

In joining the Volscians, Coriolanus thus does not betray Rome out of a sense of petty revenge but regains his integrity. His only act of betrayal occurs at the end when, instead of leading the Volscian army into Rome, he organizes a peace treaty, submitting to the pressure of his mother, the true figure of superego Evil. This is why he returns to the Volscians, fully aware of what awaits him there: the well-deserved

9   Che Guevara, *Guerilla Warfare*, Lincoln: University of Nebraska Press 1998, p. 173.

punishment for his betrayal. And this is why Fiennes's *Coriolanus* is effectively like the eye of God in an Orthodox icon: without changing a word in Shakespeare's play, it looks specifically at us, at our predicament today, portraying the unique figure of a radical freedom fighter.

Let us elaborate on this idea a bit further. If, as we have already noted apropos of *The Wire*, the Hegelian *Weltgeist* has recently moved from cinema to TV—or, in more secular terms, if they are the hegemonic ideological medium—how come that they are dominated by the figure of the sociopath? Adam Kotsko has recently explored a whole panoply of such "sociopaths we love": mobsters like Tony Soprano, serial killers like Dexter, torturing anti-terrorist agents like Jack Bauer, up to primitive dysfunctional fathers like Homer Simpson.[10] What unites all of these characters is that, for whatever reason (from simple subjective satisfaction or desire for material profit up to protecting the basic fabric of our society), they are able, without any moral qualms, to suspend the basic rules of human concern and decency, cheating, killing, torturing, manipulating, humiliating, etcetera, their neighbors without constraint. How are we to interpret this weird fascination? The obvious answer would have be to read it as an index of the failure of the social bond that holds our society together: this society obviously needs sociopaths if it is to function "normally"; only they can save it, that is, society's rules have to be broken for the sake of society itself. But Kotsko's perceptive analysis takes a crucial step further: the problem with these sociopaths is that *they are not sociopathic enough*; they still need society and, in their own way, serve it. In other words, what Lacan calls the "big Other" remains operative, determining the goals that motivate our sociopathic heroes (social success, wealth, justice, public safety), and it also easily incorporates the effects of their actions (House and Bauer do save many lives, and so on). From this basic dialectical insight, Kotsko outlines the idea of a *true* sociopath as a social revolutionary effectively questioning the basic coordinates of society's big Other. Kotsko identifies the redeeming features of every important type of sociopath he describes: the "schemers" display a kind of innocent childlike joy in their plots to screw over their friends;

---

10   See Adam Kotsko, *Why We Love Sociopaths*, Alresford: Zero Books 2012. A more detailed analysis would have to mention the predecessors of such "sociopaths we love" in literature and cinema, from Patricia Highsmith's Tom Ripley to Thomas Harris's Hannibal Lecter.

the "climbers" display exceptional creativity and a willingness to take risks in the ruthless pursuit of their goals; the "enforcers" (McNulty, Bauer) are dedicated to a goal more important than normal life with its pursuit of happiness. Does not the combination of these three features provide the perfect model for an authentic revolutionary? He is ready to forsake his life for his cause; he brings to it creativity and a readiness to take risks; and, last but not least, he finds an innocent joy in his activity, clear of all traces of sacrificial masochism.

In 1929, when a journalist asked Stalin what characterized a good Bolshevik, his answer was a combination of Russian dedication and American pragmatic spirit. Today, eighty years later, one should add to the list innocent joy: what we need is a subject who combines the dedication of Jack Bauer, the inventive pragmatic spirit of Stringer Bell, and the innocently malicious joy of Homer Simpson.

CHAPTER TEN

Conclusion: Signs From the Future

So where do we stand now, in 2012? 2011 was the year of dreaming dangerously, of the revival of radical emancipatory politics all around the world. Now, a year later, every day brings new evidence of how fragile and inconsistent that awakening was, as the signs of exhaustion begin to show: the enthusiasm of the Arab Spring is mired in compromise and religious fundamentalism; the OWS movement is losing momentum to such an extent that, in a nice case of the "cunning of reason," the police cleansing of Zuccotti Park and other sites of protest cannot but appear as a blessing in disguise, covering up the imminent loss of momentum. And the same story is repeated around the world: the Maoists in Nepal seem outmaneuvered by the reactionary royalist forces; Venezuela's "Bolivarian" experiment is increasingly regressing into a caudillo-run populism ... What are we to do in such depressive times when dreams seem to fade away? Is the only choice we have between the nostalgic-narcissistic remembrance of sublime moments of enthusiasm and the cynical-realist explanation of why these attempts to change the situation inevitably had to fail?

The first thing to say is that the subterranean work of dissatisfaction is still going on: the rage is building up and a new wave of revolts will follow. The unnatural relative calm of the spring of 2012 is more and more perforated by growing tensions announcing new explosions. What makes the situation so ominous is the all-pervasive sense of blockage: there is no clear way out, and the ruling elite is clearly losing its ability to rule. Even more disturbing is the obvious fact that democracy isn't working: after elections in Greece and in Spain, the same frustrations remain. How should we read the signs of this rage? In his *Arcades Project*, Walter Benjamin quotes the French historian André Monglond: "The past has left images of itself in literary texts, images comparable to those which are imprinted by light on a photo-sensitive plate. The future alone possesses developers active enough to scan such surfaces perfectly."[1] Events like the OWS protests, the Arab Spring, the demonstrations in Greece and Spain, and so on, have to be read as such signs from the future. In other words, we should turn around the usual historicist perspective of understanding an event through its context and genesis. Radical emancipatory outbursts cannot be understood in this way: instead of analyzing them as part of the continuum of past and present, we should bring in the perspective of the future, taking them as limited, distorted (sometimes even per-verted) fragments of a utopian future that lies dormant in the present as its hidden potential. According to Deleuze, in Proust "people and things occupy a place in time which is incommensurable with the one they have in space": the famous madeleine is here in place, but this is not its true time.[2] In a similar way, one should learn the art of recog-nizing, from an engaged subjective position, elements which are here, in our space, but whose time is the emancipated future, the future of the Communist Idea.

However, while we must learn to watch for such signs, we should also be aware that what we are doing now will only become readable once the future is here, so we should not put too much energy into a desperate search for the "germs of Communism" in today's society. What is needed, then, is a delicate balance between reading the signs from the (hypothetical Communist) future and maintaining the

---

1   Walter Benjamin, *The Arcades Project*, Cambridge: Belknap Press 1999. p. 482.
2   Gilles Deleuze: *Cinema 2: The Time-Image*, Minneapolis: Minnesota University Press 1989, p. 39. With all respect for Marcel Proust's genius, when one reads about his way of life—spending most of the day in a half-darkened room, sleeping much of the time, his dependence on his servant—it is difficult to resist the pleasure of imagining him being condemned by a workers' regime to a year or so in a re-education camp, where he would be forced to get up at 5 AM, wash in cold water, and then, after a meager breakfast, work most of the day digging up and transporting earth, with the evenings filled up with singing political songs and writing confessions.

radical openness of that future: openness alone ends in a decisionist nihilism that impels us to leap into the void, while taking the signs of the future for granted risks succumbing to the temptation of determinist planning (we know what the future should look like and, from the position of a meta-language somehow exempted from history, we just have to realize it). However, the balance one should strive for has nothing to do with some kind of wise "middle way" avoiding both extremes ("we know in a general sense the shape of the future we are moving towards, but we must always remain open to unpredictable contingencies"). Signs from the future are not constitutive but regulative in the Kantian sense; their status is subjectively mediated; that is, they are not discernible from any neutral "objective" study of history, but only from an engaged position—following them involves an existential wager in Pascal's sense. We are dealing here with a circular structure best exemplified by a science-fiction story set a couple of hundred years in the future when time travel has become possible: An art critic who becomes fascinated by the works of a New York painter from our era decides to travel back in time to meet him. He discovers that the painter is a worthless drunk who even goes so far as to steal the time machine from him and escape into the future. Alone in today's world, the art critic paints all the paintings that fascinated him in the future and prompted him to travel into the past. In a homologous way, the Communist signs from the future come from a place that will become actual only if we follow these signs—in other words, they are signs that, paradoxically, precede that of which they are the signs. Recall the Pascalian topic of *deus absconditus*, of a "hidden god" discernible only to those who search for him, who are engaged on the path of this search:

God has willed to redeem men and to open salvation to those who seek it. But men render themselves so unworthy of it that it is right that God should refuse to some, because of their obduracy, what He grants others from a compassion which is not due to them. If He had willed to overcome the obstinacy of the most hardened, He could have done so by revealing Himself so manifestly to them that they could not have doubted of the truth of His essence; as it will appear at the last day, with such thunders and such a convulsion of nature that the dead will rise again, and the blindest will see Him. It is not in this manner that He has willed to appear in His advent of mercy, because, as so many make themselves unworthy of His mercy, He has willed to leave them in the loss of the good which they do not want. It was not, then, right that He should appear in a manner manifestly divine, and completely capable of convincing all men; but it was also not right that He should come in so hidden a manner that He could not be known by those who should sincerely seek Him. He has willed to make himself quite recognizable by those; and thus, willing to appear openly to those who seek Him with all their heart, and to be hidden from those who flee from Him with all their heart. He so regulates the knowledge of Himself that He has given signs of Himself, visible to those who seek Him, and not to those who seek Him not. There is enough light for those who only desire to see, and enough obscurity for those who have a contrary disposition. (*Pensées* 430)

God gives us these signs in the guise of miracles, which is why they are characterized by the same mixture of light and obscurity: miracles are not visible as such to everyone, but only to believers— skeptical non-believers (to whom Pascal refers as "*libertins*," in a typical seventeenth-century sense, as opposed to the predominant eighteenth-century meaning of debauchery) can easily dismiss them as natural phenomena, and those who believe in them as victims of superstition. Pascal thus openly admits a kind of hermeneutic circle in the form of the mutual interdependence of miracles and "doctrine" (Church teaching): "Rule: we must judge of doctrine by miracles; we must judge of miracles by doctrine. All this is true, but contains no contradiction" (*Pensées* 842). Perhaps we can apply here Kant's formula of the relationship between reason and intuition: doctrine without miracles is sterile and impotent; miracles without doctrine are blind and meaningless. Their mutual interdependence is thus not symmetrical: "Miracles are for doctrine, and not doctrine for miracles." In Badiou's terms, "miracle" is Pascal's name for an Event, an intrusion of the impossible-Real into our ordinary reality that momentarily suspends its causal nexus; however, it is only those who take up an engaged subjective position, subjects who "desire to see," who can truly identify a miracle.[3]

Many perceptive Marxists have noted how this topic of Pascal's, far from being a regression to obscurantist theology, points forward

---

3   As to the relevance of Pascal's *deus absconditus* for the notion of transference in psychoanalysis, see Guy Le Gaufey, *L'objet a*, Paris: EPEL 2012.

towards the Marxist notion of a revolutionary theory whose truth is discernible only from an engaged class position. And are we not today in exactly the same situation with regard to Communism? The times of "revealed Communism" are over: we can no longer pretend (or act as if) the Communist truth is simply here for everyone to see, accessible to neutral rational historical analysis; there is no Communist "big Other," no higher historical necessity or teleology to guide and legitimize our acts. In such a situation, today's *libertins* (postmodern historicist skeptics) thrive, and the only way to counter them—to assert the dimension of the Event (of eternal Truth) in our epoch of contingency—is to practice a kind of Communism *absconditus*. What defines today's Communist is the "doctrine" (theory) that enables him to discern in (the contemporary version of) a "miracle"—say, an unexpected event like the uprising in Tahrir Square—its Communist nature, to read it as a sign from the (Communist) future. (For a *libertin*, of course, such an event remains the confused outcome of social frustrations and illusions, an outburst that will probably lead to an even worse situation than the one to which it reacted.) And, again, this future is not "objective"; it will come to be only through the subjective engagement that sustains it.

Perhaps we should turn the usual reproach about what we want and what we don't want around: what we want (in the long term, at least) is basically clear; but do we really know what we don't want, that is, what we are ready to renounce of our present "freedoms"? We want coffee, but do we want it without milk or without cream? (Without a state? Without private property? and so on.) It is here that we should resolutely follow Hegel, whose opening towards the future is a *negative* one, articulated in limiting statements like the famous "one cannot jump ahead of one's time" from his *Philosophy of Right*. No wonder Hegel formulated this same limitation apropos politics: as Communists, we should abstain from any positive imagining of the future Communist society. Recall Christ's skeptical words from Mark 13 against the prophets of doom: "If anyone tells you, 'Look, here is the Christ!' or, 'Look, there!' don't believe it. For there will arise false Christs and false prophets, and they will show signs and wonders, that they may lead astray, if possible, even the chosen ones. But you watch."[4] Watch for the signs of the apocalypse, bearing

---

4   Also translated as "Be on your guard!"

in mind that the open meaning of this term in Greek, *apokálypsis* ("lifting of the veil" or "revelation"), is a disclosure of something hidden from the majority of mankind in an era dominated by false-hood and misconception. On account of this radical heterogeneity of the New, its arrival cannot but cause terror and confusion—recall Heiner Müller's famous motto: "the first appearance of the new is the dread." Or as Seneca put it almost two thousand years ago: "*Et ipse miror vixque iam facto malo / potuisse fieri credo*" (Although the evil is already done, we still find it hard to believe it is possible [*Medea* 883]). This is how we react to radical Evil: it is real, but still perceived as impossible. But does the same not hold for everything that is really New?

So what about the apocalyptic tone we often hear today, especially after some new catastrophe has occurred? The ultimate paradox here is that today's excessive catastrophism (the mantra that "the end of the world is near") is itself a defense mechanism, a way of obfuscat-ing the real dangers, of not taking them seriously. This is why the only appropriate reply to an ecologist trying to convince us of the impending threat is that the true target of his desperate plea is *his own non-belief.* Consequently, our answer to him should be some-thing like "Don't worry, the catastrophe will come for sure!—the impossible is already happening all around us; but, watch patiently, don't succumb to hasty extrapolations, don't indulge in the properly perverse pleasure of thinking 'This is it! The dreaded moment has arrived!'" In ecology, this apocalyptic fascination takes many diverse forms: global warming will drown us all in a couple of decades; bioge-netics will mean the end of human ethics and responsibility; the bees will soon die out and global starvation will follow … Take all these threats seriously, yes, but don't be seduced by them or wallow in the false sense of guilt and justice they invite ("We offended Mother Earth, so are getting what we deserve!"). Instead, keep a cool head and … "watch":

> But you who watch, keep awake. For you do not know when the time will come. It is like a man going on a journey, when he leaves home and puts his servants in charge, each with his work, and commands the doorkeeper to stay awake. Therefore stay awake—for you do not know when the master of the house will come, in the evening, or at midnight, or when the rooster crows, or in the morning—lest he come

suddenly and find you asleep. And what I say to you I say to all: Stay awake. (Mark 13)

Stay wake and watch for what? As we have already seen, the Left entered a period of profound crisis—the shadow of the twentieth century still hangs over it, and the full scope of the defeat is not yet admitted. In the years of prospering capitalism, it was easy for the Left to be a Cassandra, warning that our prosperity is based on illusions and prophesizing catastrophes to come. Now the economic down-turn and social disintegration the Left was waiting for is here; protests and revolts are popping up all around the globe—but what is con-spicuously absent is any consistent Leftist reply to these events, any project of how to transpose islands of chaotic resistance into a positive program of social change: "When and if a national economy enters into crisis in the present interlocking global order, what has *anyone* to say—in any non-laughable detail—about 'socialism in one country' or even 'partly detached pseudo-nation-state non-finance-capital-driven capitalism'?" T. J. Clark sees the reason for this inability to act in the Left's "futurism," in its orientation towards a future of radical emancipation; due to this fixation, the Left is immobilized "by the idea that it should spend its time turning over the entrails of the present for the signs of catastrophe and salvation," that is, it continues to be premised "on some terracotta multitude waiting to march out of the emperor's tomb."

We have to admit the grain of truth in this simplified bleak vision, which seems to undermine the very possibility of a proper politi-cal Event: perhaps we should effectively renounce the myth of a Great Awakening—the moment when (if not the old working class then) a new alliance of the dispossessed, the multitude or what-ever, will gather its forces and master a decisive intervention. So, what happens if we radically renounce this stance of eschatological expectation? Clark concludes that one has to admit the tragic vision of (social) life: there is no (great bright) future. The "tiger" of suffer-ing, evil, and violence is here to stay, and, in such circumstances, the only reasonable politics is the politics of moderation which tries to contain the monster: "a politics actually directed, step by step, failure by failure, to preventing the tiger from charging out would be the most moderate and revolutionary there has ever been." Practicing such a politics would provoke a brutal reply from those in power and dissolve the "boundaries between political organizing and armed resistance." Again, the grain of truth in this proposal is that, often, a strategically well-placed precise "moderate" demand can trigger a global transformation—recall Gorbachev's "moderate" attempt to reform the Soviet Union, which resulted in its disintegration. But is this all one should say (and do)?

There are in French two words for "future" which cannot be adequately rendered in English: *futur* and *avenir*. *Futur* stands for "future" as the continuation of the present, as the full actualization of tendencies already in existence; while *avenir* points more towards a radical break, a discontinuity with the present—*avenir* is what is to come (*a venir*), not just what will be. Say, in today's apocalyptic global situation, the ultimate horizon of the future is what Jean-Pierre Dupuy calls the dystopian "fixed point," the zero-point of the ecological breakdown, of global economic and social chaos—even if it is indefinitely postponed, this zero-point is the virtual "attractor" towards which our reality, left to itself, tends. The way to combat the catastrophe is through acts that interrupt this drifting towards the catastrophic "fixed point" and take upon themselves the risk of giving birth to some radical Otherness "to come." We can see here how ambiguous the slogan "no future" is: at a deeper level, it does not designate the closure, the impossibility of change, but what we should be striving for—to break the hold of the catastrophic "future" and thereby open up a space for something New "to come."

Based on this distinction, we can see a problem with Marx (as well as with the twentieth-century Left): it was not that Marx was too utopian in his Communist dreams, but that his Communism was too "futural." What Marx wrote about Plato (Plato's *Republic* was not a utopia, but an idealized image of the existing Ancient Greek society) holds for Marx himself: what Marx conceived as Communism remained an idealized image of capitalism, capitalism without capitalism, that is, expanded self-reproduction without profit and exploitation. This is why we should return from Marx to Hegel, to Hegel's "tragic" vision of the social process where no hidden teleology is guiding us, where every intervention is a jump into the unknown, where the result always thwarts our expectations. All we can be certain of is that the existing system cannot reproduce itself indefinitely: whatever will come after will not be "our future." A new war in the Middle East or an economic chaos or an extraordinary environmental catastrophe can swiftly change the basic coordinates of our predicament. We should fully accept this openness, guiding ourselves on nothing more than ambiguous signs from the future.